# HOPE AS OLD AS FIRE

## A Spiritual Diary

*By Steven Charleston*

RED MOON PUBLICATIONS
Oklahoma City, OK 73120
www.redmoonpublications.com

Cover Art by Suzanne Charleston, www.suzanneartist.com

Copyright © 2012 by Red Moon Publications

Library of Congress Control Number: 2012903497

ISBN 978-0-9851419-0-5

Printed in the United Sates of America

# Dedication

*To My Family*
*To Suzanne who never gave up on me*
*To Nick who keeps me honest*
*To Choc and Billie who gave me life*

# JANUARY

## January

At the beginning of the year 2011, some friends encouraged me to join Facebook, the global social network online. For those who may not be familiar with Facebook, imagine that you have an electronic bulletin board on which you can write or post whatever you want. People put up messages to family or friends, photographs of their children or their travels, videos of music or movies, political commentaries: the choices are endless.

Staring at that blank wall for the first time I did not know what to do. I am not an extroverted commentator on life around me, but an introverted contemplator of the life within. My spiritual practice is to wake each morning at 4:00 a.m. to meditate and pray. So I started posting the impressions that surfaced in my mind, in my heart, when I prayed. Without realizing it, I began to keep a spiritual diary.

At first, only a handful of people were connected to me on Facebook. Only a few ever read what I wrote. But through word of mouth online, more and more people began to join my page. They began to stop by each day to read my meditations. Eventually, so many ask me to collect these thoughts into a single volume that I decided to do so. This book is the result.

What you will find here is a vision that is as personal as it is eclectic. I do not have a story to tell or a message to impart. I have only the daily revelations of one human being trying to make sense of the mystery we all share, the mystery of being alive.

## January

Some of these meditations will speak directly to events. Many of the meditations, however, arise from a more timeless space, from my own wandering into the thin air of the spirit. There is an Index at the back of the book to help you navigate between these different impressions and give you a sense for how they evolved. You will see that some dates may be "missing" in the diary. These were the Saturdays I took off from writing to open a space for prayer requests from the community that has grown up around the meditations.

Because Facebook restricts the number of words a person can use (and changes those restrictions from time to time) the meditations vary a little in length, but they all required a poetry of purpose to condense emotion into a few lines. You may read them as symbolic. Your interpretation is as valid as my meaning.

The diary is divided by months. This preface of explanation is January because it was only in late January that I signed on to Facebook. It was on February first that the real diary began. You can read these entries day by day, or you can roam through the days, finding entries that may speak to you where you are. However you read this spiritual diary, I hope that you will read it as a gift of blessing, for that ultimately is why I created it. I have been blessed by God through many quiet mornings of prayer. I have heard things, seen things, felt things that helped me make my spiritual life more real and my real life more holy. I hope you have that same experience.

# FEBRUARY

### February 1

Here is a message in a spirit bottle, tossed onto the electric sea of online. If you happen to pick it up as it drifts by, it is meant for you: "the answer you seek in prayer can be found in the memory you treasure most."

### February 2

O God, please protect all the peoples of Egypt and Tunisia, whatever their faith or cause, and give them the peace that is the midwife to their freedom. Do not let the light of liberty be stillborn, but breathe life into it through your Spirit, that justice may grow where only oppression dug the graves of hope.

### February 3

The great engines of history, operated by the few, grind out their products of pain, to the cost of the many. Against them, whole armies cannot stand. And yet, you and I have entrusted to our care a single word that can confuse their purpose and slow their advance, even stop them completely if we speak our word as one. Shout peace into the winds of war.

**February 4**

Some of our deepest prayers are prayers for healing. Healing is not a shallow pool that we pray over like skipping stones, as if simple repetition alone could charm us an answer. Healing is a deep well where only the most ancient waters of life lay hidden, waiting for the one who will brave the dark to drink.

**February 5**

We all bear the soul scar of a wrong done to us for reasons we still have trouble untwisting from the dark threads of pain washed memory. I offer no quick cure, but take this to use when you need it most against the long held hurt: close your eyes and feel the warm hand of One who was there and loves you all the more for what you have endured.

**February 6**

Anybody out there need a John 15:11 card? I am handing them out free today. Just put it in your pocket or purse. Then, when you think things couldn't get worse, take it out, press it against your heart, and let its warmth run through you like a stream of liquid sunshine.

**February 8**

There is someone close to you who shelters your soul with a love that may be strained but never broken. Knowing you for who you are, this one loves you still and, by so doing, shares with you a source of strength beyond measure. Turn to see this beloved again and do not let the sun go down without some small gesture to the gift they have been.

**February 9**

In the vanity of my heart I have believed that there are some things I have done for which I can never, should never, be forgiven. Like dark pearls of pain I have worn these thoughts around my neck for all the world to see, hoping for respite in shame if not mercy. But God follows me, whispering all the while, you are forgiven, even if you pretend you are not. The pearls are only my faux faith.

**February 11**

Like me, have you ever worn "busy" as a mask? Like smoke and mirrors my hamster wheel distracts me from feeling the longing within, the fear without, that others will notice. Won't the music keep playing as long as I dance? Our first taste of redemption is the permission God gives us to simply stop.

**February 12**

Here is a blessing for any who pass by and see themselves in this mirror of hope: Yes, you made a difference. Yes, your life has mattered. Yes, the price you paid was sufficient to the good you were able to do. Yes, someone has noticed and cared. Yes, God intended it so. Needed it so. Your faith made it so. Yes.

**February 13**

Name one cultural institution in which you have complete confidence. I ask the question of myself but received only silence for my answer. There is no system to save us. Not our educational system, not judicial, not governmental, not scientific, not health care. In this flawed age, only you, O God, are the ground steady beneath our feet.

**February 14**

The vision of love is to see the beloved as God sees, not blind to the imperfections, but focused on the moments when kindness transcended self-interest, when care came in just the right words to mend a bruised heart, when in a timeless touch you knew together you could weather any storm chance might bring your way.

**February 15**

How often I have stood undecided I cannot count, but as if in a dream I keep returning to the crossroads, both paths dark before me, praying for a light to follow. The answer is not to be found by staring into your mind, but by feeling the hand unseen on your shoulder. Intuition is made sacred by trust.

**February 16**

I have a smile to share because I have just encountered a mini-angel. Not one of the big, wings like a 747 mega messengers, but a small fry hummingbird of the heavenly host who darted in to see if I could use any help. Her job is to do a little light cleaning of old hurts or current worries. She did a great job too. I feel much better. Lighter. Hopefully happy. Can I send her your way?

**February 17**

Something sacred this way comes, summoned by the prayer you have said so many times in the secret places of your heart. A longing prayer, whispered against all the odds, something you half believed could never happen. It is to that dream that change takes wing. Something sacred this way comes. Be awake for already it crosses the horizon of hope.

**February 18**

Beneath the starlight have I been humbled, when all my houses of cards were revealed, and the tight grip of control slipped from my hand unable to fend off even the common cold. I cannot command the seasons of my life or measure the meaning of change. But I can stand beneath the starlight and trust the One who makes me shine through even the darkest night.

**February 19**

I have seen the faces. Faces flickering like fireflies. From Egypt and from Wisconsin, both near and far, flickering on Twitter, the online night of a single voice crying freedom into the electronic void. I shout back solidarity and wonder if hidden hands will pull the plug before we recognize the same face in the mirror of history.

**February 20**

Come stand with me on a wilder shore, where age is no impediment to dreams, and life begins anew each dawn, as the Spirit inspires through whispers in your ear. We are not bound by illness or chained to clock-like time, but swell with such a future in our hearts, jealous Death cannot contain it, even if one day he try.

**February 21**

Power is a vanity that narcotic pride feeds on crystal pain, an addiction for those so hunting of approval they have become predators of their own kind. Along the holy path do not fear lonely struggle, truth is a solitary traveler. Fear applause too loud for you to hear your own heart. That siren song sings sorrow.

**February 22**

For all the times I have broken, betrayed or battered, even within the safest haven I have called home, and thought myself lost, lost in a sea of sorrow beyond rescue: I have been lifted up by strong hands and healed of every hurt, by the One who teaches me to use my pain as strength for lifting others.

**February 23**

Did you ever wake up to feel the Spirit wind blowing all around you? Blowing away all doubts and dark dreams, all clinging anxieties and lumbering fears. Sweeping away feral illness and lifting the body light to be washed in a breeze of wholeness. At dawn this day She made her way past my window. Shall I bid her find you as well?

**February 2 4**

I built this roadside shrine, beside the online highway, where weary travelers could rest, if only for a moment. Within its cinnamon scented air, where the skirts of bells catch the breeze and candle light dances with shadows, there is a single book on which, by miracle, each traveler finds their name. Its message opened reads always the same: you are loved.

**February 2 5**

If like sacred spies we could pass unnoticed on a busy street, and I could slip into your hand a message, a single word, a word that would be a key to unlock your mystery, and bring you an answer to prayer, would you brave all doubt to receive it, trusting your life to the One who sent it? Then open your hand now and behold the grace of God.

**February 2 6**

There is a grove where orphaned dreams, abandoned before their time, are paper lanterns, each with a name written on it. They glow beneath dark branches hanging, fading into twilight. I have walked there many times: praying one dream to return to the heart that lost it. Can you read a name you know? Pray for the dream of another before the evening of hope fades beneath dark branches hanging.

**February 27**

Do not read these words unless you are willing to accept them and stand responsible for their meaning. To you, authority has been given to work a wonder in another life. To you, authority has been entrusted to shape a new reality. Be accountable for that gift. Use it with wisdom, aware and intentional, and arise a healer, both born and blessed.

**February 28**

My ancestors are watching over me, I see their faces in a million stars, watching silently through the night. Their spirits move beneath the moon. Will I keep faith with their last hope, to honor the Earth that bore them? Or will I bend to cold hearted greed, and leave none to mourn them? My ancestors are watching over me as yours watch over you. Tell me now, tell me now, which choice will we show them?

# MARCH

**March 1**

There is a grace to life that cannot be taught but only revealed. It comes from patient kindness and a willingness to wait. It puts the other first and is not too proud to please. It prizes gentleness and shares a soft embrace. This grace is within us all, though hidden by insistent culture. It is a gift we can only find, when we give it to another.

**March 2**

I dreamed we all had wings, not in heaven but now, spread wide in many colors. We soared and swept, circled and spun, delighting in freedom. Old limits were gone. Gravity lost its hold. The air was our home and a vision vast opened before us. Imagination is the gift of wings. It lifts us to see what God will show us. If only we will trust our faith to rise from familiar ground to test the winds of wonder.

**M a r c h   3**

I cry comfort in a manic age, when agendas are armies, marching in terror, trailing compassion in the dust, a fallen banner of a fallen people, the poor whose only growth is in numbers. I cry comfort in a callous age, where children are profit, women are barter, and elders expendable, all lost in the Twitter of Empire. When the weak are forgotten power spreads silence to smother its rivals. In that silence I cry comfort.

**M a r c h   4**

Will you pray with me for the man who needs a job? For the woman looking for work? No eloquent words, no deeper meaning, just a flat out appeal: O God, give work today to those who need it. Do not let them see the sun set once more on their hope, but come quickly to fulfill it, by giving them the dignity of a fair wage, and the honor to simply earn it.

**M a r c h   5**

L
ast night I saw a stray, limping away from city streets, a bone skin dog alone, seeking shelter in the night. I could not stop, caught in traffic current, but felt such sadness, I vowed in prayer to cast this call. God's creatures are our family. Their care our charge from the One who made us all. Love them. Help them. And when you do, remember once you were stray.

**M a r c h   6**

A
s a child I believed I had an angel guardian, who with wings widespread watched over me, night and day, with gentle care unceasing. Now that I am grown, I have seen life's struggle for what it is, I carry the scars to prove it. I am more convinced than ever that my child faith was innocent truth. God does send love alive to us all. Close your eyes. Hold your breath. You can hear wings rustling round you.

**M a r c h   7**

Draw in the breath of peace. What you face will be resolved. What you need will be supplied. What you hope revealed. Faith is your strength. Do not worry or waver. Peace in heart and mind, body and soul, enfold you. Peace, deep peace, surround you. Breathe in as if you were God's first creation. Breathe in life and breathe in healing. No matter where you walk today, you walk in peace unfailing.

**M a r c h   8**

Behold, the quiet time comes. Like twilight, its deep shadows spread, stilling frantic life with a cool hand of calm. Be still now. Be quiet. Call within for ancient thoughts to arise, give them room to simply be. Wisdom is a well where sacred waters reflect the face that watches, reflect the moon, untroubled by winds of ceaseless change. Be still. Be ready. The quiet time comes.

**M a r c h   9**

I know I will make my return one day, out beyond where the wild wood ends, across an old stone bridge that spans the thin place stream, between here and home. I neither long nor dread to take this path. It is in time of its own. I wait between loves old and new, with my task before me. When the moment of journey begins, I will know, for my pockets will be full of stardust, my steps light as first falling snow.

**M a r c h   1 0**

S omeone hears in secret, the whispers of the heart, that fly on broken wings, messengers without destination, seeking answers in the dark. Speak a single prayer, one you treasure most. Release your hope. Watch it take flight. Then wait in sanctuary, in the evening of your soul, for an answer sailing free on wings restored, by grace beyond all measure.

**M a r c h   1 1**

Though the Earth be moved, and mountains shake, and all the seas recoil, the care of God will never fail, to find frail life, where it may be, and shelter innocence, beneath unchanging love. Pray mercy. Pray protection. Pray for all in peril. If our prayers save one soul, comfort one heart, mend one shattered life, let us bend our spirits to the task and steady the ground beneath us with faith the sure foundation.

**M a r c h   1 2**

Rescued. I have been rescued. Saved, pulled up, found, given another chance. Cool intellects shy from it but warm hearts embrace it. How many feel it today? Still alive. In the aftermath of loss. In the shock of rescue but still alive. There are no words, O God, no words to say how that feels. To be safe in your arms. To live another day. Undeserving but safe. In your arms. There are no words, O God. Only tears.

**March 1 3**

How hard to live in anxious times, when pixeled pain surrounds us, streaming feed of struggle, flashed in sorrowed news, never ending. Hurt, hurt they say, all is hurt around us. Within this storm I may stand weak, only a fragile thing, a single soul, but I have a God graced voice. Life, life I cry into the electric night, life, hope and healing. Into the black wind I shout, love, deep love, love never ending.

**March 1 4**

Listen. A whispered voice rides the wind, one you have heard before. It speaks to you even now. It calls outside your door. Listen. I am not its herald, only the doorman to dreams, who lets a wild wind rush in, scattering your papers on the floor, a breath of needed change. Listen. Your thoughts are sails, unfurl your hope and fly the wind, far from comfort's hold.

**March 15**

I heard you pray again last night, though you never knew it. Elder hearts need less sleep. They hear a thousand prayers, of a thousand voices speaking. Grandmother God descended, gathering prayers in a starlight apron, hands ancient in the craft of love. I looked away, for if our eyes meet, my time bound watch would end, but I held up your prayer, to join so many, in Her deep care keeping.

**March 16**

I looked and saw a glowing shroud against a dark horizon. Children ran while parents wept and elders huddled helpless. Fear is a toxic brew swept on poison air. Before it courage pales and edges to the brink of flight. If we link our lives in prayer protecting, we can drive this danger back. God calls us now to work as one, all our fears to face. Do not turn away but accept this day with heart as strong as grace.

## March 17

For one among us a message in a dream: On my journey home to you, I am far nearer than you know, near enough to see you there, waiting where you have waited, waited for so long. Patient is the longing heart. Unsleeping the eyes that watch. What you have needed most can be seen clearly now, if only you will look again, not in the direction you imagined, but toward a distant star, a question never asked.

## March 18

I will stand beside you. Against all odds. Come what may. Smile if you want. I am broken, ragged around the edges of my tattered soul, a Don Quixote for your champion. But I am pure of heart, my prayers arrows of light flying through the darkest night. I will stand beside you. I believe in you and in my believing lies strength enough to make mountains move. As long as I draw breath, I will stand beside you.

**M a r c h   2 0**

Nicodemus came by night, beneath a watching moon, trailing shadows with every step, hiding his hope like guilt. Nicodemus flew by night, beneath a clear light moon, his robes made sails, his beard a pennant, lifted on a wind that caught him by surprise, scattering his hope for all to see. Now hear a mystery: by nightfall the burden you bear will weigh a feather's weight, if you hear love singing, singing in the wind.

**M a r c h   2 1**

I awoke today to see our first sunrise. Many generations hence, in a peaceful place, scholars will wonder, when did humanity first rise, to cry enough is enough, putting an end to greed and war? Was it not a woman of Japan, dirty and tired, who stood to sing, sing defiant love, until her song circled the Earth, singing a garden from ashes? When did history change? They will never know. But we know. We see the dawn.

### March 22

Icome, O God, to this lonely place, far from the crush of daily care, to tell you a truth: my spirit has grown tired. A flame of faith too often used, I have dimmed the light within. Renew me. Restore me. Rest me. Let me run again. If this is your prayer, find a still space, open your hands to receive, breathe deeply the light you seek. Breathe love and renewal for a warm hand wants to touch your heart.

### March 23

Irise a new creation, as old sorrows fall away, bright shining in my strength, alive with love renewed. I walk in beauty, certain in every step, my hand a healer's hand, all I touch with grace endued. Confident heart, undoubting mind, this miracle of life redeemed. I have a mission to share, not just the good I do, but the good I am, the good God made me be. Blessed, a blessing I become.

**M a r c h   2 4**

Midnight. I just awoke, feeling someone cry out in need. I stretch out my spirit, like radar sweeping, sweeping in search of that place of pain. A lonely man in a cheap motel? A child in a hospital bed? Where are you? Can you feel me as I feel you? Can you tell you are not alone? O God, my seeker's prayer please answer, for two of us, two midnight souls, strangers with radar spirits, each in search of you.

**M a r c h   2 5**

One cold night, a village girl, not yet fifteen, cradled her belly when the thought came clear: this child of mine will be special. She did not know why, she only believed it was so. Like every woman, she believed in her child. Like every woman, she believed in hope when hope was not to be seen. Today I am a wing bent angel sent to say thank you to Mary. To every woman. Thank you for the gift of your great faith.

**March 27**

I drove home on lonely roads, along the Milky Way, to find the whole Earth sleeping, at the dawn of a new day. No triumphant return, no honors won, just a quiet step, from one world to the next. I am on the right path, as long as I do not pretend that I know where I am going. We journey together, you and I, on lonely roads along the Milky Way, love the language of our wisdom.

**March 28**

I walked among lost graves, to hear my ancestors speak, whispering beneath the branches, as the timeless wind passed by. The faith we leave is the faith we live and that the faith we learn. Some seek the teacher's role to hide an emptiness within. Others listen, listen to truth among the poor, see truth amid the weak, touch truth on bodies broken, and know truth, as the timeless wind passes by.

**M a r c h   2 9**

S ophia is a playful child, a girl with mischief eyes, who dances before us, leading us with laughter along the way. Thinking wisdom a ponderous thing, we may miss her simple signs. Look up. Be alert. Along your path her message waits, hidden in plain sight. A stranger's word, a chance event, a vision common but clear. If Sophia you seek, a spiritual surprise, then put dance in your step and mischief in your eyes.

**M a r c h   3 0**

T rust me as I trust you. Let us exchange trust, here, beneath the wings of God. No covenant more sacred, no words more soul worthy. Love moves without bidding, a river that knows no bounds, but trust is deliberate love, love tamed to purpose. It is a gift given once, steel strong and sparrow soft, whose loss is more painful, than freeing a life to die. Trust me as I trust you, here, beneath the wings of God.

**M a r c h   3 1**

I will not cede to sorrow the territory of my life, hard won hope, bought and paid for, by labors of faith, by more soul stretched nights than I can count. All about me I hear the whole creation groan, as if redemption had abandoned the field, leaving cold pain alone to rule. My love is stern in stubborn joy, my arms strong enough to hold a thousand prayers. If you need light take my hand, for I have light to share.

# APRIL

**A p r i l   1**

Yesterday life brought bad news and laid it at my door, like an abandoned infant placed in my care. Sometimes we receive what we do not ask, or want, or need. We are given burdens when we have burdens to spare. A holy life is not lived in constant calm, as if the soul were an Ark afloat on a still sea. I am not measured faithful because I am free of care, but become faithful when orphaned care finds me unafraid.

**A p r i l   3**

How beautiful you are to me, there are no words to convey. Each time I see you for the first time, how you steal my breath away. You are the work of the One whose art is beyond measure. A self portrait of all that is pure and generous, an image incarnate of love. You are fashioned of stardust and moonlight, of songs only angels know. When I see you, love bows its head. How beautiful, how beautiful you are, to me.

**A p r i l   4**

In heaven on high, a hand unseen turns a page, and your life changes. How much of life is spent changing? Waiting for change, surprised by change, riding change like white water through an uncertain canyon. Change comes as it will. Be patient if it is slow. Be balanced if fast. In all things know change for what it is: your teacher. Do not be afraid for the Changeless One never turns a page without purpose.

**A p r i l   5**

How much does a soul weigh? We know. We have held one in our hands. As parent, friend, confessor, or lover: we have at times been entrusted with the soul of another. A newborn soul weighs less than a cloud. A sorrowful soul weighs the weight of the world. We are soul bearers. Stewards of the souls of others. Be worthy of your calling. Let your soul not be a burden nor shun the soul of another in need.

**April 6**

Grim Puritans in party hats, bunkered Cardinals with balloons, powerful Primates playing tag. Moses brings the message, from Sinai on high, lighten up God commands, let my laughter go. If you find nothing funny in faith, you may have missed the joke. Heaven is not the refuge for the pious and the prim, but a playground for all God's children, who have learned from their Teacher, how to live and laugh again.

**April 7**

To all who live in struggle, to all who struggle to live, hear clear the holy Word that comes for you this day. You have felt invisible, trying hard to try. You have brave-faced hidden worry, painted smiles on all your ghosts. But those days die in new light descended. Look up to see Grandmother God stretch out her hand of love. In boldest faith, your release I proclaim, your struggle at last ended.

**A p r i l   8**

In a sleep stolen night, I heard a murmur of many voices, voices ancient and wise, speaking just beyond the walls of time. Across the eternal sea, where those we love find rest, messages are passed, like nets of light, cast to catch a listening heart. Can you hear it? Someone you loved loves you still and deep comfort seeks to send. Be still. Heaven speaks, when we need, if only in faith, we will pay heed.

**A p r i l   1 0**

Lazarus sleeps within us all, a private hope buried away, a dream to be reborn. Children imagine a new world each day, until age tricks the mind to entomb imagination, in places dark and confined. Roll back the rock of youth resigned, call life from castles in the air, let your playful spirit run free, create what you cannot see. Remember, Lazarus sleeps until you chance to dream.

**April 11**

O God alone in your high heaven, do you ever feel lonely like me? If you do, then hear my prayer, for all who watch from windows, waiting beside phones that never ring. Unloved teens, adults left longing, elders sitting alone in rooms: for all citizens of the Big Empty I ask a single grace. Let them be discovered today, like the fine jewel they are, the treasure of someone's heart, wished from a smaller star.

**April 12**

C ome sing a song of sunrise, come dance before the dawn. Last night a voice familiar whispered while I slept, a message of meaning for the one meant to hear. You have kept watch to see this day, so long and so long alone, waiting with dimming hope, your only companion prayer. Rejoice. Your waiting is at an end. Look up: joyful news walks on winged steps. Rejoice. Sing now your sunrise. Dance before the dawn.

**April 13**

I stand to celebrate my church. Come, stand with me. When holy houses become bunkers, and the wars of faith rage, fear closes gates to refugees, while judgment stalks the stage. How brave a thing, in times like these, to have doors wide open. To love without condition. To reconcile and not condemn. I stand to celebrate my church, this weather worn light, that still shines so brightly, through the darkest night.

**April 14**

O God, thank you for the weavers of wisdom, the mentors of our lives. These great women, these good men, are your grace embodied. They are guides Spirit sent, teachers of lessons no book could contain, healers of healers. I see them now, both here and above, with wreaths of light encircled. I honor each one. I bow my head in gratitude enduring. They have shaped us, as they served you, your truth's legacy ensuring.

**April 15**

Like leaves tossed by wind, our lives fly before us. Days rush past, harried commuters, hurrying, hurrying, to catch the train of time. Years are masks, we seem to change, before the bathroom mirror: when did we get so gray, when did the kids get so big, when did when pass us by? Multitaskers, speed-dialers, life-racers: stop. Gently stop. The meaning of it all is never found at the end, but only along the way.

**April 17**

The word of truth comes our way, and beckons us to follow. Not with pious promises, not with banners of power unfurled, but with humble resolve, a destiny to embrace. Pain lies beyond those gates, all shouts of joy subdued, but love will have its day, and not let life be denied. Truth walks a path many proclaim, but only a few will follow. It shares a bitter sweet cup that makes death's threat hollow.

**April 18**

For all who have never seen the Easter light, let us hold high a single candle, a beacon of invitation. Remember, the light came not for those in dawn but shadow. We have walked this way before, but for others it is a detour uncertain. How many have no idea of what we do or why? Can we count them? Before I step into the warmth, I will recall the cold, for I once knew how precious a thing, a single candle could be.

**April 19**

On this day in 1995 the hand of evil placed a bomb in our city that took the lives of 168 innocent people, 19 of them children under 6 years of age. Our church is only a block away and was severely damaged. I have been asked to pray this morning at the memorial. Please join me. Pray today for all innocent victims of terror. Pray for an end to violence against children. I know they are listening.

**April 20**

We are keepers of a great mystery, stewards of a sacred trust. Each morning we inherit our bright realm, each night we float on its dark sea. We live. Simple as that. We live. It is the being-ness of the thing that matters. The gift of another day, the dream of tomorrow. Take not for granted nor waste a moment so fine a favor as God has shown. Live your mystery: you breathe and you know it.

**April 21**

Do not dread the dark door that leads to a moonless shore. There are footprints to follow, by the One who first found the way, along the beach to the house beside the sea. Those you love will greet you, with a sheltering embrace, no cold wind will find you, all sorrow saved by grace. You are a barefoot child who walked wet sands of time, to laugh as God wipes clean your toes, before Her hearth everlasting.

**A p r i l   2 2**

On this day birds refuse to fly, the wind folds its wings, the sea grows calm. No bell rings, no baby cries. On this day clamor ceases, stillness a silent shroud, to cover sound in breathless waiting. The child of life, the son of hope, lover of all pure love, has died. Died most cruelly. On this day hang your head, grieve as though grief were new, for goodness itself has gone away, and peace passed into death.

**A p r i l   2 3**

Dwell we now in darkness deep, our pledge of faith in God to keep. It is not easy to be transformed. It requires trust and patience. If we rush to Easter, denying the death of change, we make it magic, not rebirth. We rest now in the womb of God, Her miracle to become. We wait without control, without the need to know. We surrender life to Her, that life may be remade, by the same light She used, when She made us all.

**April 24**

S he comes running, running still sleeping streets, hair flying, heart pumping, running to share her news. She enters wild eyed, breathless with wonder: the stone is rolled away. I believe her. In her eyes a light no other has ever seen. Fear falls to the floor, morning air fills my lungs. And I start running. Running the sleeping streets, running to chase the dawn, running to share the news. The stone is rolled away!

**April 25**

T hey say shamans fly. Me, I just float. Out over housetops, drifting on the night wind, watching the world sleep. I hear the prayers of good hearts, rising on currents of hope, to circle the vesper Moon. I see the angels keep ceaseless rounds, nightshift nurses with violet wings, outspread to shelter those in need. Be at peace. Rest in peace. Prayer covers you. Angels guard you. God loves you. All through the night.

**A p r i l   2 6**

L et us speak honestly, you and I, of the hard work faith can be. If it feels like a greeting card, we may not be doing our job. Faith takes us where we do not want to go, to be with those we do not want to meet, to do what we think we cannot do. It is not comfort achieved, but comfort given away. Let us speak honestly, you and I, for we never work alone, but serve God's great union, faith workers, paid in prayer.

**A p r i l   2 7**

O ut in the desert, a shrine still stands, tended by silent monks, who guard its single treasure: the mirror of Solomon, the eye of God. It shows a reflection but once, without sin or sorrow. It reveals you as God sees you, an image of eternal love. When you are in doubt, search out that shrine, believe in who you are. You are the face of love, for all the world to see, and so you were made, and so you shall ever be.

**April 28**

There is a plague among us, striking down working families, the silent death of their hopes, worried sick by an ill economy. Homes are lost, jobs are scarce, elders live in fear. We are pumping our kid's college into the tank of our car. I pray God, help those in need and cure the greed that makes the great divide grow deeper. Drive back the plague that haunts our homes. Restore us with your justice.

**April 29**

Have mercy, O God, on all whose lives have shattered beneath the fury of dark winds twisted. They join the growing list for which we pray in the aftermath of natural disaster. Mother Earth writhes in pain, the whole creation groaning. Our care for Nature must match our care for all God's children. A holy harmony we must restore. Let life in balance be that life from pain may be set free.

**MAY**

**M a y  1**

I speak a word of respect to those who strive for justice, who still believe in what is right and true and good and work to make it happen. We live in an age that does you little honor, an age that smothers courage with complacency, that wants us to look the other way. In such times the few herd the many while the poor pay the price. Thank you for confronting power to witness to what makes us free.

**M a y  2**

Vengeance is a cold hand that takes but cannot give. In the arc of night I saw shrouded figures standing on parade by a grave. Their testimony burned my heart, though never a word was spoken. Their truth a somber love, of lives lost and broken. Hate for hate never ends war's endless dance. We do not regain the fallen with more of what took them. Justice gives birth to peace. Revenge is barren.

**M a y   3**

Now face we an uncertain day. Fate stands afraid. Instant news bears instant doubt, threads of worry weave a net, resolve wavers in a dark wind. At the hinge of history we awake. Rise up you saints of peace. Fear not. Behold the sun at our back, the Spirit carries our banner. Peace it proclaims, peace it praises. Our strength runs like a river, hate and terror shall not win this day. Rise up you saints of peace.

**M a y   4**

I am praying with you. In the early hours, when the Earth is hushed, and even songbirds sleep, I wake to search for you, my pledge of prayer to keep. I imagine all you hope, breathing the rhythm of your soul, as you and I in silent faith, stretch out our hands to God. I do not know how our asking will be answered but answered it will be. I am praying with you, and Someone is listening, listening, to you and to me.

**M a y  5**

I speak for the quiet ones, for those who cannot speak for themselves. The woman who walks for water, the man who sleeps on a street. The child crying from hunger, the family whose crops have failed. Beneath the shout of great events, the poor are left unheard. Voices stolen by the storm. I speak for the quiet ones, for the poor of every land. Look! Over here! See into the eyes that speak what no word will ever say.

**M a y  6**

I am a follower of the chubby Jesus, the Messiah who loves to eat. I know his image is long and lean, but that is a mistake. His work began at a wedding and followed through many a meal. With loaves and fishes he made sure we all ate our fill. At a last supper he told us the banquet must go on. Oh, cadaverous Christians of beady eye, who doubt that faith is fun, come to the feast of God, who shares the bread of life.

**M a y   8**

To honor all, I honor one, the girl who bore the Savior. She held him first at fourteen, held him last at forty-five. Bookends of love and loss, a sacred journey, from child to leader, walked the woman's way, with courage and with compassion. Daughter of the land. Voice of the poor. Mother of hope eternal. Holy Maryam give your grace to sisters of your story. To honor one, we honor all: the women who bear the world.

**M a y   9**

Love as though it was your last day, with a heart unguarded in affection. Let no hurt contain you, but claim the high mountains of your spirit, a radiant freedom to forgive flowing from you like first light. Be the kindness you were born to be, the mercy for which you were made. Love as though it was your last day. For if you live as if you were in heaven, you will know why God eternal life has given.

**M a y   1 0**

In every life there is a tangled love, a relationship complex in the emotional math of pain. It did not start out to be so, but there it is, layered like ancient earth, layered with memories, the deep sediment of a broken heart. Pray with me for all who struggle to forgive, to understand and to heal. Untangle the histories of our hurt. Let light fall along a path too long left in shadow.

**M a y   1 1**

Do not be silent when you have such a story to share. Beside you gray draped throngs walk with weighted steps a long walk alone. Their joy a passing day. Their strength made of money. Their hope an acquisition. They do not hear freedom speak for fear empties their language of blessing. Do not be silent, but witness to what you know. The life of another may wait on your word.

**M a y   1 2**

Change rides winds of time, moving all before it. It may come as a breeze, gently swaying our reason, or toss us as a storm, into an unexpected season. Though we build barricades of tradition, change subverts  pride, exposes purpose, opens past, to release the seeds of tomorrow. Change is the mind of God, doing the work of creation. Life to come from life passing. The process we name eternity.

**M a y   1 3**

You are forgiven. You are free. You are loved. You are accepted and received, brought out from  obscurity, to stand beneath the hand of blessing. You have been seen and heard, understood and embraced. You are the center of a heart whose compassion is wider than the widest sea. You are who you are by holy design, made to rejoice, to live like one forgiven, one set free, one loved. You are.

## May 15

For seekers I have a message, dream given to impart, a note for the holy nomad, practitioner of love as art. Your search is who you are. You found the answer when you took your first step: wisdom is not in the knowing, as if wisdom was a prize, but in the doing, when you gain what you give, and give what you gain, the meaning in grateful eyes. Travel in peace. Your search is your gift. And your search never ends.

## May 16

I've stayed with Jesus all these years because Jesus has stayed with me. Beneath the intellectual trimmings and poetic sentiment is the core of earthy experience. Jesus didn't dump me even when I deserved dumping. God's love saw me through the kind of hurts you don't forget. Plain talk for plain faith. Simple truth for honest hearts. God's love is real. Prayer works. Faith heals. I can't say it better than that.

**M a y   1 7**

I sat talking of things past, with old friends who knew me then, and for just a moment, a flicker of time-light, those memories lived again. Blessed we are by friendships that never fade: a never ending stream, water of life, to nurture lives left living, in the dry lands of a lonely mind. God bless those who stand beside us, who accept us as we are, who love us for no other cause, but that we share a common star.

**M a y   1 8**

Wake up. I hear something. The sound of Spirit. Coming this way. Coming on the rush of wings. Listen. It draws closer. With every breath it moves on currents of prayer. Wake up. Be alert. This power knows your name. It calls you with intimate grace. It whispers an echo of your heart. Wake up. Your moment has come. Spirit hovers before you. Speak. Life is yours. Even angels await your word.

**May 1 9**

God bless the church: our traveling tribe, our motley crew, caravan of the conflicted and courageous, stumbling toward paradise, the hurt and the hopeful, wounded healers, singing along the way. Life within her tents is never easy, but life without her would be darkness beyond our imagining. Bless the church, dear God, your quarreling brood, your stubborn flock, your love living for love, your dream of what might be.

**May 2 0**

Life spilled out across the floor, like coins falling from a pocket, without purpose or direction. Love bartered in ever smaller pieces, lost in the giving, lost in the search for affection. Some stories are acted out for all to see, some hidden in deep layers of shame. To all twilight souls, I offer a faith to trust, a place to stand and heal, a family that knows your name.

**May 22**

I have been praying for a woman on her vision quest. Alone she sat through the night, beneath the wind and stars, singing her chant to Grandmother God, praying for all creation. In her song she held us in her spirit. Her breath our breath, her prayer our prayer. When all is said and done, we are what we are willing to give. I honor all who give of themselves, that we may pass in peace, beneath the wind and stars.

**May 23**

I am giving out Indulgences. In the 16th century they were sold, but that caused a little trouble, so I offer mine for free. My Indulgence is not a pass to Heaven but a ticket to fun. It grants my episcopal blessing for you to indulge yourself. Get off the hamster wheel. Do something just for you. Eat ice-cream. Take a nap. Read a book. Rest. My Indulgences celebrate this: being comes before doing. May I give you one?

**M a y  2 4**

The turn of my heart bends toward you, O God, my longing a desire almost beyond bearing. I search for you in infinite stretches of imagination. I discover you in intimate spaces of need. You give my wounded spirit shelter, my restless life purpose, my questioning mind the embrace of wonder. I pray today all who are lost may find you, as I found you, waiting with love more patient than time.

**M a y  2 5**

Grandmother God, I pray for all who struggle today to rebuild their lives. Survivors of earthquakes or storms. Those who search for jobs or face divorce. People who cope with illness or grief. For all who strive to pick up the pieces and start again. With your strong hands repair what is broken, reshape what is hurt, remake what is lost. With your grace create again life from dust, joy from ashes, songs from sorrow.

**M a y   2 6**

I will take the night shift of your prayer. I will keep watch while you sleep. I will be the light glowing in your darkness, the quiet harbor of your dreams. Be at peace. Be not afraid. All will be well. Though we pass this night in mystery, uncertain to know the last soliloquy of our lives, what we do know beyond all doubt, is that we will face the dawn together. Rest now. I have the night shift of your prayer.

**M a y   2 7**

Vmmona ka Anumpa hvt ahanta mvt: in the beginning was the Word. Listen. Each word you speak is ancient in power. It can heal or hurt, bind or free, create or destroy. This arrogant age breaks the wings of language, to cage words in bytes it swallows. You know better. The Word abides hidden from control, an authority undiminished by machines. Listen. That authority is within you. You have only to speak to release it.

**M a y  2 9**

I pray the gift of a patient spirit. Even though I live in an age that demands an instant answer, I have found a different rhythm to follow, one ancient and deep, a rock steady beneath my feet. Trust will bring you what you need. Trust will take you home. Trust in time becomes peace. Take this word to your heart, let it in your spirit abide: do not be anxious but certain, for God knows and God will provide.

**M a y  3 0**

For all the fallen, in all the wars, through all time, on every side, whose families waited, whose spouses prayed, whose children cried, who marched off, never to return, and now are only remembered. I do not make heroic what happened to you, for war is an ugly thing, but I honor your humanity, your sacrifice and your loss, your right to be. God bless you all. God forgive us for losing you as we did.

**M a y   3 1**

L ove comes to us, abides in us, transforms us, becomes us. Love finds us in hidden places but dances with us in public. Love lives in quiet but shouts our name, even if only we can hear it. Love fills any space we will make, follows any direction we will take. Love waits for an eternity to share one moment's grace. Love is who we are, when we are, what we are, as love first imagined.

JUNE

### June 1

Open the eyes of your soul, behold the light that shines all around you. This is not the fancy of the poet's mind, the soft language of the sages, but a reality as clear as insight itself. Hearts darkened by pain, fear or sadness need the warmth of living light. You are that light. When you believe, you see. When you hope, you enlighten. When you touch, you warm. Live the light you are. You are the light you live

### June 2

The Buddhists have the prayer wheel, a cylinder inscribed with prayers, sending out those hopes each time it is turned. Imagine the Earth is such a wheel, circling endlessly, as all around it, in every place and hour, someone is praying, sending out love or longing, a wheel of ceaseless prayer. If God sees us from a distance, our little blue wheel spins with faith, as it prays eternally throughout the whole creation.

**J u n e   3**

Nothing lasts. Of all we learn on our passage to wisdom, this truth is most haunting. Nothing lasts. All we know and have, all we see and touch, all we imagine and wish, slips like sunlight between the clouds. What wonder then to know, this fear is but illusion, change but a dream. God waits for us to wake, children of a new morning, to find all is where we left it. A promise made with a kiss from our Mother before we fell asleep.

**J u n e   5**

I pray for all who seek wisdom. How often we stand before the tests that try our souls, uncertain which answer to claim. How often we count our own insights but guesses, advice a stream babbling over stones. Come deep Spirit of God, come to those who need you, give them the blessing of your mind. Whisper wisdom into their ears, let their eyes see clearly, that your direction is revealed, that they follow you more nearly.

**June 6**

Busy as this day may be, there is a still-point within it. As time runs by like a river racing to the sea, the Spirit creates quiet pools, small islands, spaces to break the single-minded movement. Find one of these today before you white water over rocks. Even a small silence can calm your soul. Sit in peace. Close your eyes. Breathe. See how the water wears sunlight like diamonds, shadows like a shawl.

**June 7**

Some measure the sacred by a rosary of rules. Some read the Scriptures with tweezers. Some claim to have locked truth in the basement. Some can count the saved on one hand. But truth cannot be contained. God runs barefoot past the sign that says "Keep Off The Grass". She has friends who raise eyebrows and has been known to give away her lunch money to the old lady in the park. God is not some but all.

### June 8

The dry season is coming. Pay heed to my word, please, pay heed to what you feel. Sniff the wind. Watch the birds. Taste the earth. The deep pools of our art are fewer now. The rivers of grace run dry. The healing rains have drifted south. The dew falls thin on ground longing for living water. The heat of fear is a drought of love and all who need justice go thirsty. Look up. Time to move. The dry season is coming.

### June 9

I prayed for a young boy. He was facing something very hard, but his eyes were steady with hope. Courage is not always a grand display, but comes most often quietly. It is the choice to stay, to be, to care, the choice to love at all costs. We each have our moments of strength, when we stand for what we believe, offer what we have, try as best we can. God bless all silent heroes who are so brave as to walk by faith.

**J u n e   1 0**

Here is a pocket blessing. Carry it where you go. Use it when you need. It has no shelf life, weighs nothing, fits comfortably where it is placed. Hope in a handbag. But don't let looks fool you. It is small but has wondrous power. Take it out for healing, protection, comfort. It will not fail to help. It is guaranteed with a lifetime warranty. And if you give it away, I can always replace it. Free of charge.

**J u n e   1 2**

If you have obstacles that block you from your journey clear them from your path with prayer. God is a contractor, a builder and an engineer. With the tools of the Spirit, there is no job too great or too small. Focus the energy of hope and any problem will move. Apply love as a lever, and all weights will shift. Work with God. Make straight the path of your life. Believe and it will be.

### June 13

I have walked beneath the Northern Lights, when the air was so cold it could break, talking to God with streamer white words, down a village path, far from the resorts of vanity. I have sat with God on a city roof, alone among the millions, steel fish swimming the cold currents of traffic, rushing to rush again. God is in all places, at once and everywhere, as distant as the Moon, as near as the nearest prayer.

### June 14

What mind designed the sunset? Dreamed the Himalayas? Drew the Nile with a finger? Imagined the dance of dolphins? We serve a God of great art, whose canvas is the sky, opening each night in the gallery of endless stars. We serve the sculptor whose clay is the Earth, whose shapes are endless in variety. To craft such beauty, how much more beautiful still, the heart that first conceived it? What mind saw color before color was born?

**June 15**

Guilt and I are old friends, having spent many long hours together. Guilt tells me how worthless I am. I confess new and deeper faults. In the end guilt leaves promising to return. I wave farewell, glad guilt is gone but too tired to move. I slouch toward my bed. But just as I reach the stairs, God's forgiveness comes bounding down, child-like with innocent acceptance, leaps into my arms and makes my soul weightless.

**June 16**

I may only be a speck of dust, floating in a universe vast, but I am a very interesting speck. I intend to make some waves, even if they be as small as me. I will bring a speck's worth of love to life, a speck more of hope, a speck more of laughter. I will add a speck of compassion, to tip the scales of creation, toward the side of every speck who seeks mercy. A speck of dust I may only be, but a speck of light is still light to those who sit in darkness.

**June 17**

Iam healed when I heal. I am made whole by the joy I
share. I am enriched by what I give away. I am
strengthened by my weakness, when that weakness is lifted
up on the palm of prayer. I come first when I am last to
receive. I am not afraid, even when fear finds me in the
wave tossed sea. I am born when I die. I am the image of
God when God is visible in every face I see. I am the leader
who follows, the master who serves the servant. I am what
I am for the I AM that caught me to make me free.

**June 19**

Last night I saw a blessing pass me by, on its way to a
stranger. I did not know who was to be blessed or why,
but I could feel the warmth of the kindness intended. We
live in a world of faces, most we never see, who are hidden
chapters, in a story we all share. There is no human who
has ever lived, or will live, to whom I am not related. God's
kinship is a bond of blessing between me and all who
breathe. I am those I know as well as those I fear. I am the
other to myself, the self in every soul I see.

**June 20**

I am older now than when the fires first burned brightly on a distant hill. I have seen more. Hurt more. Learned more along the way. Age is a dance between frailty and freedom. Now my mind can stretch while my body cannot. But before the last word of my song is sung, I will make such a music of my soul, that even angels will look up, to see who could so praise the Ancient of Days.

**June 21**

O God, give your grace through me. Take my measure of blessings, for I have more than I need. Let it tip the scales of hope for a woman waiting, for a man praying, for any child crying. Take my portion. Surprise someone. Let my giving a true gift be: grace offered without condition. Let love live another day, where love may be least expected.

**June 22**

As coins are counted in another room, our debt to the Earth grows. As votes are counted in another room, our debate continues. Is global warming really true? Are the oceans dying? Are these storms only chance? Is the ice melting around us? It is a magician's hand that shows us nothing wrong. The last illusion we self-create tells us our island is not sinking. Time now to stop talking. Time to do what must be done. Time to save our home.

**June 23**

Why do I believe? What keeps faith alive? Loss and grief, struggle and disappointment, like rain on rock they wear faith down. I believe not because I am wise or strong. I am neither. I believe because I have seen the God who walks beside me. There is no journey God has not taken. No hope God has not shared. I believe not what I have been told, but what I see, a love that never departs, a love that believes in me.

### June 24

Come sit with me beside a pool of wonder. Take time to watch still water. See how deep your mind can go, when you drop it like a stone, into hidden depths of the heart, where even reason cannot follow. We will never know every answer. Our task is to be stewards of the mysteries of God, in awe of what we have yet to learn, mystics beside the pool of living water, where shadows are as welcome as the sun.

### June 26

The voice was given to you. Before you took breath, it was given to you. It is not words alone, but voice, power spoken. With it you can comfort and heal, lift up, create and convince. As the voice of God commands the stars, so your voice may order the planets of your heart's desire. Take care with so great a gift. Use it wisely. Speak what must be said, say what others long to hear. The voice was given to you.

**June 27**

On one act of kindness, a whole life can turn. In a single moment, a soul may be restored. Our lives are not crafted from great dramas alone, but shaped by the small asides of life, the unscripted encounters, that teach us to be who we are. Be mindful of the fire that fills you. Let it warm but never burn. Speak kindly, touch lightly, hold gently. The casual remark for you is destiny for another.

**June 28**

My peace I give you. With those words the breath of God passed over us and abides with us still. No matter how frantic the engines of need drive us, how layered the problems, how great the challenge, we have a core of faith. Peace. Deep, certain, steady. Peace is your birthright, peace your natural home. God's peace within, God's love without, you are sheltered in the everlasting arms, the heart of all that hopes.

**June 29**

You are never more than a step from love, no matter where you go. No distance can separate you from the touch of grace, no depth conceal you from the care of the One who made you. You walk in light. Go then to the places that need you. Step over thresholds of hurt for the sake of others. Dare to be the truth, share the work of justice. Even if to save a few you lost it all, you would not count the cost.

**June 30**

Last night I heard a voice, speaking on ribbons of wind, whispering a holy promise, broken lives to mend. I will act on that word. I will claim a promise of wholeness for any who are broken. For one or many, for any or for all. I send my prayer as a blessing to ring the wide world round. The power of the Spirit, carried on ribbons of wind. Be healed. Be whole. Be free. Be the quiet dawn you never expected to see.

# JULY

**July 1**

Think back to the girl you used to be, the boy you once were. That bright and innocent light still shines, deep within your being, a star constant in goodness, a God made mind, just awakening. No years can steal the memory of memory's origin, when backyards were twice their size, and toys the tools of wonder. Childhood is not our past, but the beckon of our future.

**July 3**

One more day. God gives me one more day. With each sunrise I see, God gives me one more day to make right what is wrong, to open what is closed, to find what is lost, to be what I long to become. I can work miracles today. I can change the course of history with a word. In these few hours I have the chance to shape time itself into timeless love. One more day. That's all I need to live one day as if it were eternity.

July 4

When the waiting grows long, I will stay with you. I know what waiting is all about. I have waited for many answers, over many years, to many needs. I have sat in hospitals, beside phones, in empty churches with only the sound of my prayers to mark the time. Do not confuse time with love. Waiting itself is holy. God will provide. The answer will come. Until then, I will stay with you, just as you have stayed with me.

July 5

If you were not here, the song of life would be diminished, the symphony of light and stars would dim, the rush of the wind would grow still, the laughter of children fall to a whisper. You are not here by mistake or chance, but by the purpose of the One who made you. You are living hope, sent by God to share love to all the world. You are blessing embodied. If you were not here, none of us would ever be the same.

### July 6

When two or three are brought together, around the challenge that is God, a small flame arises. A word of truth, of healing, fans that flame to fire. For God's own good reasons, this space has become a hearth of gathering for many of us. For how long, I do not know. So warm your soul while you can, there are storms enough for tomorrow. Take this light when you go, that a flame may arise, where only darkness dwelled.

### July 7

I slept last night in peace, sheltered in the arms of God. I awoke in peace and pray now in peace, a spring of living water, flowing through silent streets, out into the city, beyond to all the world. If there is a troubled heart, I know my love will find it. I am a source. A place of beginning. The peace God gives starts here, with me, in all I say and do. I am peace today, and so good friend, are you.

**J u l y   8**

I want to save someone today. I want to save them, not convert them. If we Christians are in the saving business then there is work enough to do. Countless women and children are traffic moving on a dark highway, bought and sold, used and discarded, by men who have lost all feeling. Countless more are battered and abused in their homes, innocence smothered in silence. Yes, I want to save someone today. How about you?

**J u l y   1 0**

Here is a simple message: God loves you. In spite of it all, through it all, God loves you. There is no shadow so deep that it can hide you from this light, no illness so strong that it can steal it away, no maze of worry that will keep it from you. All else may change, but this one thing is ever true, you never stand alone. You are never forgotten. Never. God loves you. The rest is just a story.

**July 11**

Every journey begins with where you have already been. Within each of us there is an internal map, drawn by the hand of our own experience that tells us where to go in life, and how to get there. All the boundaries are neatly marked. Age, gender and class. Just follow the lines. Or you could toss the map. Forget the lines. Make the journey a discovery. Take the risk. Lose the map. Follow the compass God gave you.

**July 12**

We each have a miracle within us, perhaps more than one. We may not part the waters, but we can do something so inspiring, so loving, that it sets in motion acts of generous kindness that roll through time like music dancing on air. You will know when the moment comes, to touch life with purpose. You are a steward of God's power, a source of love so deep, it can bend the hand of hope, to touch the least of these.

**July 13**

Saints play in the sand. Doctors climb trees, scientists play tag. Novelists watch cartoons, economists ride the swing. The president is fussy in the grocery cart. The senator wants a new toy. All around me the citizens of another day are the children of my time. God grant them peace, where they can be what they were born to be: children of God, watching old dreamers like me, resting in God's shade.

**July 14**

I do not ask for God's presence in my life because I am an empty mind waiting for truth. Faith is not the absence of critical thought, but thought put to the greatest question. We were made to reason, to wonder, to ask, for only by these gifts do we discover the far reaches of God's imagination. Church is not a court, but a laboratory. We were not made to conform, but to explore. Even doubt may be a door.

**J u l y   1 5**

Ihave survived broken dreams, lost chances, and disappointments in abundance. I have weathered the storms of my soul and made the long walk out of sorrow. I am veteran enough of life to know life can hurt. Therefore I do not see faith as soft sentiment to wash away the worry. It is made of stronger stuff. Do not be afraid but trust in what you believe. Life can not invent a problem that you and God will not solve.

**J u l y   1 6**

There are no strangers. In the house of Grandmother God there are no empty chairs. All who seek shelter are welcomed. All who are hungry are fed. No one is turned away, no one questioned, no one made to wait. Love is offered freely to any, to every, to all. Diversity abounds in this household, a tribe of many clans. Every language spoken, every family at home. If we are not all there, none of us have arrived.

**July 17**

My life is not the stuff of high religious drama. I do not live the saintly life, far removed from mundane matters, but dwell down here with the dirty dishes. With monthly bills, sneezing kids, and an old car that runs mostly on prayer. I do laundry. I clean toilets. Not the stuff of legend. I need help in my chore-filled life, grace my routine to renew, a God who always stays late, to help on the clean-up crew.

**July 18**

Jesus is a Ninja. The Virgin Mary is green. Those camels look like dragons and I think Noah's ark has hit an iceberg. St. Peter has wings. Elephants came to the first Christmas. At Jesus' baptism, the dove fires lasers out of her eyes. Over the years I have seen some wonderful paintings of Bible stories in the mixed media of crayons and love. I think all the artists deserve a prayer today. God bless them each and every one.

### July 19

Open your heart today. Be alert. Be ready. When the Spirit moves, she moves on dancer's feet. Her change sweeps in like fresh wind from the sea. Do not believe that change will never come or may have passed you by. It rushes round you while you sleep, it moves life while you slumber. Wake up to find good news waiting at your gate. Wake up to see the pattern. An answer right before you, a blessing at your door.

### July 20

Regrets are stones, carried for penance against the memory of deeds badly done. Some are small grains of loss. Others rock hard hurts of great size. I have carried my fair share, taking them with me when I move, storing them in the back alleys of my heart, aware that mistakes seem eternal. But now by the place I pray, on God's holy ground, the earth is littered with stones. Some small. Some large. All left behind.

**July 21**

I sit listening to the prayers of a woman beyond the reach of age. Her hair is winter white. Her voice Earth old. As we sit praying in her small house, deep within her hills, I feel the Spirit rise, rise on wings of fire. I am among my people. I am within my Tribe. Every word I speak now is healing. Every act, an act of mercy, older than the hills that seek to hold our prayer.

**July 22**

Come be strong with me today. Come stand beneath the Spirit. Perhaps like me you have troubles enough to fill your day, a life that has taught you limits. Perhaps like me you have no power but God's good love, no wisdom apart from learning. But faith is found among those who know the meaning of moving mountains. When I rise nothing can contain me. Come be strong with me today. Come stand beneath the Spirit.

**July 24**

Solemn the silence around me. I have come to listen to what God may say, to hear ancient love recited, a sonnet from the author of dreams. Be still and listen, be still and listen. Lay down your cares like knitting, take up quiet contemplation. Be still and listen. God is speaking ten thousand ways, in ways without language. Be still and listen. Take time to hear what has never before been spoken.

**July 25**

I come empty handed to help you. I have no power or position, no wealth or pull. I am uncertain of what tomorrow holds, and hopeful that I can make this day through. We are a funny pair, we two, with strong hearts, but weak hands, an unlikely place to place a bet. But we have this in common, a faith unbowed and unbroken. So cheer up. Nothing can stop us now. Just point me to your mountain. We've won before we've begun.

**July 26**

Today I will be the answer to someone's prayer. Today I will be a word of hope. Today I will delight a child, comfort a friend, embrace a stranger. Today I will help. My spiritual life is not measured by the abstraction of my mind, but by the concrete way I use my life, and use it today. Today is my piece of eternity given by God for a reason. Today is my infinite blessing made possible in my finite time.

**July 27**

The same great power that moves the stars, that orders the seas and sets the winds in motion, that gives birth to all that lives and makes the Moon rise in pale beauty, this same power stands by your side. You need never fear. You need never doubt. The One who designed all you see knows your name, and loves you with a love as deep as love can find.

**July 28**

Who needs your prayer? Who waits out there, wondering what the next day will bring, wrapped in worry, unsure of how to feel? The answer is beyond counting. You are the unseen source of hope for people you know and for many you will never meet. You, the source, for so very many. Your prayers reach their darkest corner. Your faith makes their life work. Who needs your prayer? We all do.

**July 29**

I pray for the working poor, for families in need, for those who feel financial sand moving beneath their feet. The need of money, a deep stain, colors life with worry. It steals happiness. It denies joy. I pray then for those who guide our global economy, on whose choices hang the lives of many: God, give them wisdom and compassion. Let honest work and honest pay restore the hope of your people.

**July 31**

Hear my song, you highest mountains, and all the plains below, let my voice lift up the face of trees and cause the seas to roll. I sing the glory of God. I sing the love of God, the goodness that God imparts, an endless stream of mercy flowing, ever flowing, to comfort longing hearts. Though with age my voice be old ice, cracked and thin, and my song too frail to hear, still I sing, I sing the glory of God.

# AUGUST

August 1

Receive this blessing from one who knows what blessing means: a touch of grace on a shoulder bent, by vigils kept and vigils spent. Receive the countless prayers of an older heart, the joy of a child reborn. Feel new strength in your spirit. Feel peace in your soul. All will be well, for nothing is lost, and everything found, the circle of blessing complete. I am the faith that you live, you are the blessing that I give.

August 2

Rise up good people of God, rise up and make your witness. Too long the shadows of despair have shrouded the Earth. Too long the hearts of your people have waited for dawn to be more than dread. Today is the day of salvation for all who will claim it. Let our message be a witness lived and loved: life is precious in every shape and peace the birthright of any soul born beneath the banners of heaven.

**August 3**

God help me be responsible. Help me be accountable. How often I come to you, asking you to comfort me when things go wrong, wanting to be forgiven. But stand with me through it all, when I need to see my role clearly, when I need to accept the results. There will be time then for apologies or praise. For now, hold me up, face me forward. Let me be responsible for the world I help create.

**August 4**

How great the love God has for you, no words could ever express. It is a love as boundless as the evening sky, when the first stars draw the eye to heaven. It is as lasting as time, as deep as the most hidden places of the sea. Never doubt that you are embraced by unseen arms that hold you safe against all harm. You are God's beloved, secure in the care of a love that never sleeps, where even memory cannot find you, nor sorrow steal your peace.

**August 5**

A turning point comes. I cannot tell you where or when, for each of our lives is set to its own rhythm, but none moves without change, that hinge of the heart where all that came before shifts to a new beginning. When it comes you will know it. You will feel the presence of God call you to turn, turn to new horizons. Be ready. A turning point comes, when vision is embodied, when faith becomes a choice, when what you do turns to who you will be.

**August 7**

I understand. I do not know all of the details, and the telling of them may only become a tangle, but still, I understand. I have felt like you and thought like you and prayed like you, striving against the same currents that have carried us both this far. Even if you never say a word, I understand. And on that single truth, our human story shared, we will find what we need, a life lived uniquely, but never lived alone.

**August 8**

Grandmother God, I pray energy into life today. I pray for tired souls to revive and weary spirits to renew. I pray a fresh breath, a new start, a bright idea. I pray engagement, action, movement. Wake us up, shake us up, make us up, to all that we can be. Heal us of what holds us down. Let weak resignation fall away and doubt quickly follow. I pray energy into life, your energy, the energy of a love that moves even when it is standing still.

**August 9**

Let's slip out the side door of sorrow, round past the watchman of worry, and make for the green fields beyond. Let's imagine these frail bodies can dance. Let's believe that we have all we need and more to spare. It is not pretense to play, but an act of joyful defiance against all that would hem the heart and constrain the love within. Come slip out of grim reality and find the peace that waits, in the green fields of faith, the streams of distant laughter.

**August 10**

Who is it, God? Who will it be? Which woman will take the lead? Which man will find the answer? We wait here in this fog of confusion, anxious and uncertain, wondering who will come forward to be your healing history. We wait, but the waiting grows ever harder. Please God, lift up your good leaders, inspire them with your vision, give them a hunger for justice and a heart for compassion. Set them on the new path to peace. We are ready for hope. Speak to those now whom hope has already chosen.

**August 11**

Now the harvest of blessing comes, now the fruits of faith unfold, the grace of God revealed, the healing and the kindness. Beneath all harm a goodness moves, a deep stream still flowing. It may not break forth on command, but rise up slowly, a spring of living water. Stand in your place of prayer, open your silent longing. God bends low to Earth, Her angels all attending. Pray your heart, for heaven is listening. It will be as you need. Now the harvest comes.

**August 12**

Help me with my complacency, God, help me with my indifference. Do not let me be asleep while others hurt. Keep my eyes from looking the other way. Hold me fast to the truth. Let it pierce my mind, thorns on flesh, making me uncomfortable in my privilege, uneasy in my power. Show me what I can do. Lift me up to do it. Justice in every prayer, justice in every choice, justice in every giving. Let my life be what others need.

**August 14**

How many of us see the shadows? How many of us feel the tremor? That single reed of awareness that vibrates ever so clearly when we are alert to what may come. We live in these times for a reason. God did not place us here by accident. We have work to do. We have a patch of dark to clear. If we see shadows, we are meant to see them. Without shadow, we could not be the healing light we are to this moment in history.

**August 15**

I pray healing for all who hurt, for all who struggle to regain their health. Comfort those in need, good God of mercy, remind them that they need never fear, but may always depend on your care. Help them to feel the presence of the Spirit when they are alone. Sustain them through every test and every setback. Increase their joy with good news. I pray healing, deep and lasting, healing, complete and enduring. Healing, I pray, for all who hurt.

**August 16**

God grant me this day to do what I can do. Though my contribution may be small, I want to do my share. If it is to stand and wait, then let me do so with grace. If it is to speak, then with passion and purpose. If I need to listen, then help me listen, even if to hear what I do not want to hear. If I can help, let it be so, but if I need to be out of the way, let me move quickly. In all that I do, let me be what you need me to be, that this day, I do what I can do.

**August 17**

Make way for the marching band of heaven! Just as heads are bowed, weighted by worry, a sound weaves like a thread, through the heavy air. Music. Music alive and happy, music to lift the soul. Drums beating, horns blaring, banners waving, a marching band of misfits redeemed, a ragged mob of merriment. Rejoice, rejoice, the music calls. Listen. Can you hear it? Laughing, joyous, outrageous: behold the band of heaven! They may be out of step, but never out of time.

**August 18**

We do not always get what we want, but we always have what we need. In hard times, when scarcity creeps through the mind, and fear nibbles at the edges of the spirit, it is good to remember that we are not helpless or forgotten. God supplies what we need while we wait for what we want. And though that want itself may change through time, the strength of love endures forever. Love is what we need, all we need, to turn our wants to gladness, our scarcity to abundance.

**August 19**

Dear God, bless the start of school. Bless all those of any age who walk into a classroom. Bless those who teach. Bless those who learn. Bless our intellect and our freedom. Help us remember that you did not make us to never question, but so fashioned us that we cannot stop asking, cannot stop learning. School us not to follow blindly, but to think the what and why, to search each sacred mystery, to discover what we cannot deny.

**August 21**

I am on a quest. Before this day is through, I will make someone laugh. I do not know how. But I am going to do it. I will find just the right moment, just the right joke, and the laughter will come in fits and starts, in gushes of happiness, in a quiet chuckle of delight. And why will I do this? Because long ago, a man named Jesus looked at twelve serious men with beards and thought: I am going to make someone laugh today.

**August 22**

This quiet prayer for the one who does not pray. For the man or woman, boy or girl, who may not know how to pray, but deeply needs an answer. Let me be their silent partner. Let my words speak their heart. Let my prayer give them grace, unexpected comfort and healing. Let my words become their words, giving voice to their longing, until they find the language of your love, and speak without me needing.

**August 23**

I will not leave you. Though the night is long, though storms shake the sky, I will be by your side. I will abide here in prayer, keeping watch, that you may sleep and get the rest you need. My faith will be your shelter. My love, your home. I will not leave you. Sleep then in the arms of peace. Dream a healing dream. I am with you, and will be, through this long night, until the dawn of day.

**August 24**

Caesar with a toothache. Cleopatra with an ingrown nail. How quickly our vanity turns from pride to need, from masters of fate to children with scraped knees. For all our pride we are as frail as flowers. Forgive our presumption, Grandmother God, our strut and our swagger. Forgive us our need to pretend to be in charge of what we barely understand. Give us the humility to remember that we are only children, playing make believe in your garden.

**August 25**

Mary, holy woman of our tribe, mother of many dreams, we are in need of your wisdom. Show us the path you took, with courage and devotion, that brought you to lasting faith, in a world so dark and uncertain. Remind us that the heart of a single woman, though she is without power or means, can lift the weight of history, and bend the arc of time. Mary, mother of many dreams, release your grace, that your anthem may be our own.

**August 26**

God bless the doubters, the ones who read the fine print before they sign the contract of life. God bless those who question religion and demand that it be as transparent as its teaching. Bless the ones who are not fooled by titles or claims but want to know what is being done. These voices speak a truth faith needs to hear. They hold the holy accountable, to practice what we preach. Better a doubt with integrity, than a belief without it.

**August 28**

Like so many returning home in the aftermath of a storm, there are times when we must repair and rebuild. We must restore our spirit home. Where is the damage to be found? Where are the cracks, the signs of a damaged life? Help me God, to do the work that must be done. Help me not to allow any storm to have the last word, but let me restore my life through your grace, that I may be whole, in the fair weather of your love.

**August 29**

I know when the healing comes. I can feel it move around me. Warmth like two hands touching. A sudden breeze in a room without windows. God's energy that lights the stars turned to a single touch that mends a broken child. I know when the healing comes. It comes when love has seen enough of pain. When two hands touching release an energy that fans the stars to flame.

**August 30**

You are where you are for a reason. You are who you are for a purpose. If it is a difficult moment, a joyous moment, or just a passing moment, you are part of it because you have a task to perform: you bring grace into time. Through you, God's mercy works. Through you hope and healing flow. Through you wisdom grows and lives are mended. Be conscious of your role, for without you time itself would move without meaning, and love be left to wait for the faith of another.

**August 31**

How small the world is, how very small. I could reach out to touch Africa. I could walk across the street to Asia, around the corner to Brazil. This Earth is a tiny island, floating on stardust streams. It is not the center of all that is, though people may pretend it so. It is only a little place, a back garden in need of care. Intimacy begins in imagination. Compassion in recognition. How small the distance from my heart to yours. How near the sound of your breathing.

# SEPTEMBER

### September 1

You can trust me. Few words are as powerful as these. Few promises as precious. Like a bridge made of air, we step out, walking on the faith we have in another. And if we fall, we fall far into shadow, from where we may never see this light again. You can trust me. Few words share hope as these, a healing against the lonely night, a strong arm on which to lean. And when we find this bridge, secure in love unbroken, we walk over the empty places, we run the last steps home.

### September 2

For all the great thoughts I have read, for all the deep books I have studied, none has brought me nearer to God than a walk beneath shimmering leaves, golden red with the fire of autumn, when the air is crisp and the sun a pale eye watching. I am a scholar of the senses, a theologian of the tangible. God touches me and I touch God, each time I lift a leaf from my path, a thin flake of fire, golden red, still warm from the breath that made it.

September 4

I will wait in your memory. I will wait until you need me. When that will be, I do not know. It may be after years. It may be after I am no name, on any mind, other than your own. But when the moment comes, when your life seems most in need of life, you will think of me, in this time long ago. Then my memory will be released, a last light of blessing. I will be able to help you. I will be what I once was to help you be what you will become.

September 5

The quiet struggle continues. In so many homes, the struggle for work and money continues. I will not gloss the need but pray straight to the reality: we need jobs, dear God, we need income. We need to pay our bills, set the table, fill the car, send the kids to school. Nothing fancy, nothing special, just enough to make it through the month, enough to make ends meet. Hear me please, I offer this for all who know my words before I speak: bring us work, God, and let our struggle end.

September 6

Do not be anxious if the path before you is uncertain. I have walked many roads in darkness, with only a single light to guide me. That light is trust. Walk this day in confidence, sure if not certain. God's wisdom will show you the way. God's mercy will protect you. God's strength will hold you when weary. God's joy will greet you when you arrive. Trust in God and God will always walk before you.

September 7

Love as deeply as you can for as long as life allows. Love despite chances and without reservation. Love because you were created to love. Learn to love if love is new to you. Return to love if it has been lost to you. Keep love at the center. Hold to it with tenacity, never let it go. For when life comes to collect your scattered days, you will not bend beneath regret, but count only the love that made them worth the living.

### September 8

Anger slips through the cracks. Words become liquid heat. The mind sly self-interest. Words fly like darts, no purpose other than pain. Feelings fall to hurt, the sullen quiet after the storm. Grandmother God, we cannot empty anger from our lives, but we can turn that emotion over to you. Take our anger in your cool hands. Soften it from pride to peace. Calm our hearts. Still our minds. Hold us close in your embrace until our fever has broken.

### September 9

I pray today for volunteers, for any and all who help. I pray for those who give their time and spend more hours than they have. I pray for all who do the jobs that must be done. For cooks and cleaners, office helpers, church school teachers, altar guilds and servers, acolytes and vestry members, for volunteers of every kind: a prayer of deep thanks and blessing.

### September 11

Dear God of mercy, we pray for all who died today, lost to us through acts of terror. We pray for all who gave their lives trying to save others. Give them rest and life eternal. We pray for their families. Give them comfort and the assurance that their loved ones are ever safe in your care. And for all who remain and all who remember, grant us comfort in our grief, resolve in our own defense, and most of all, the vision to find our way through clouds of war to a just and lasting peace.

### September 12

This is your day. It was made for you. Of all the recent days that have flown by like windows on a passing train, this one is meant for you. It is your time of grace. You can work your will in prayer, the course of lives to change. Take this day and use it. Spend every hour wisely. God has paused the haste of hours to grant you space to create. Make something happen. Let something happen. This is your day.

**September 13**

We cannot do it all. If we seek to lift every load, we only stumble. If we try to right every wrong, we only grow weary of struggle. If we think we can embrace every need, we only become the need ourselves. Help us, God, to remember that we are not called to be you. We cannot do it all. We are called to do what we can, when we can, as best we can, and trust the rest to you.

**September 14**

Last night I saw what tomorrow will be. Grandmother God laid her apron of starlight over the roof of the world. She sheltered creation beneath her watchful care. Wars ceased. Storms ceased. All her people were fed. Be at peace, she whispered, be healed and made new. Last night I saw what tomorrow will be. When the peace of God drifts down at night, peace rises on the red wings of morning.

### September 15

I still have trouble believing God lives next door. I thought God lived far away, in a gated community. But at times I find God shuffling around next door, early of a morning, coffee cup in hand, looking a lot like me. God waves, I wave, but this neighbor God disconcerts me with such nearness. Until I need a favor. Then I am glad God lives nearby, and is always home when needed. I peep over the fence for a chat, a time to borrow what I need, and never be asked to return it.

### September 16

Last night I saw them waiting, the children of hunger and need. The more I tried to reach them, the more they drifted away. I could not feed them all. I could not heal them all. I could not look away. Come now, God of mercy, and do what I cannot do. Spread wide your wings of shelter, bring food to hungry mouths and comfort to frail bodies, soothe and hold each one in warmth. Do not look away. They are waiting, always waiting, your children of hunger and need.

**September 18**

I search for you. With every prayer I make, with every question I ask, I search for you. I read every word I can. I study all the texts, consult the scholars. I go to the places where you have been. I walk the same streets, see the same sky, breathe the same air: but still you elude me, a mystery turning the corner just before me. God, you make me curious. God, you make me wonder. I cannot stop. I search for you.

**September 19**

Hold me close through this day, dear God, and keep me in your care. If this day brings only routine, then let even small things be done in you. If it brings the unexpected, let me deal with them with you by my side. When I speak, let it be with your words. In all things let me work for the good. Let me make these hours count the measure of my love. And when my day is done, my best the gift I have given, let me sleep beneath your wings, with dreams as pure as prayers.

September 20

With the power of prayer I strike the chain that holds any human being in the fetters of addiction. How many prisoners I see, I cannot count or number. They are each weighted with sorrow. The sounds of metal clanking out the craving that owns them. Against addiction I pray to set these captives free. Give them courage to face their truth, love to overcome it. Let them stand and walk away, their chains left rusting in the sand.

September 21

I came and knelt before you, Mary, muttering my prayers by candlelight. My words drifted out into the stillness. A prayer measured my life. I cannot say how grateful I am to know you are there. You have seen me as I am. You know me from the inside, down to the barest parts of my soul. You are always there, there by the candlelight, to hear my whispered hope. Thank you, Mary, for your gift, for the waiting and for the hearing. Thank you from one you taught to stand by kneeling.

**September 22**

This could be the moment. This could be the time when our efforts to awaken the conscience of privilege succeed, when hearts open and minds open, when fear and prejudice fall of their own dead weight. Knowing the time and place was not given to me, but surely the harvest will come. So this could be that moment, that turning point, when sorrow lies scattered beneath the feet of the poor. This day could be the dawn so many have longed to see.

**September 23**

A little illness, nothing special, just the garden variety bug, had brought me low and left me slow. How funny it seems that such a confident creature as me could be tamed so easily by a microbe. But the lesson in humility could not be more clear. As this detour into sickness runs its course, let it bring me closer to you, O God, not as my pride might lead me, but as one of your many creatures, ever dependent on you, ever in need of your care.

**September 25**

I have been in that dark garden, when there was no easy way out. I have prayed and never heard an answer. Save the one I did not want. Anger and fear in that empty orchard, denial that I had to be the one, faith wavering on the edge of courage. It is never a comfortable place to be. But there the choice is made, as it must be made, even if it is only to remain silent. Help me in my Gethsemane, as many as may come. Let me face the truth, in a garden dark, when that garden is where I must be.

**September 26**

I heard God laugh again. It was that gentle, rolling sound that starts somewhere deep inside, and then comes tumbling out in waves of delight. That laughter still echoes where God walked: around the lake, on the hillside where they ate, in the olive groves long gone. It is eternal joy, riding the wind, the first laugh, never mocking, always embracing, a healing of the soul. So I laughed too, and drew the laugh within.

### September 27

Ten points to grow a faith community: (1) embody the message you proclaim, (2) be transparent in all you do, (3) practice stewardship as a household budget, (4) laugh twice as much as you complain, (5) welcome everyone without exception, (6) expect half your plans not to work, (7) celebrate the half that does, (8) put prayer not politics at the center, (9) say thank you to others as often as you can, (10) count your blessings until they add up to miracles.

### September 28

Lift up your hearts. Be not afraid, but believing. The strength of your faith flows from a source like a river rushing to the sea. You are not abandoned to gather years too long lost, but a new creation, vibrant with a promise yet to come. Look, even angels wait upon your word, seeing in you the image of the One they serve. Draw deep the breath of courage. Do not despair of any setbacks. Your life is energy itself. Lift up your hearts: you are love made real in all you say and do.

**September 2 9**

Beware of any generation that seems lost without a leader. That search may become a dangerous thing to do. A society that is fearful, money worried, anxious for order, hungry for law, a nation of wall builders, accustomed to war, watching enemies without and enemies within, afraid its glory will fade: longing for the strong man grows, ever so quietly, while people look the other way. Help us, O God, not to flirt with forces so ancient and so evil. Rather let us put our trust in you, that justice never bends to fear nor freedom to false gods of power.

**September 3 0**

I prayed for you today. Yes, for you, though you may not believe it, thinking you are but one more face in a crowd. Even if we have never met, I see you clearly, as though you were the only point of prayer in all the world. This is not magic. It is only love, a love that sees from within. I know you. Like me you bear the marks of many long nights. Like me you hope for more than you expect. I know you. I prayed for you. And I will keep praying for you until we stand face to face, lost in grace, surprised by recognition.

# OCTOBER

October 2

Thank you, God, for the life I feel around me. For all the things that grow and breathe and stretch and move and crawl and walk and fly and swim, the great dance that circles you, the ceaseless spiral of being that winds its way to heaven. I do not know the why or how, I am not even sure of my own place in the pattern, but the dance alone is a gift, for which I will be ever grateful. So today I pray, for all I pray, for the life I feel around me.

October 3

It is greed that tilts the axis of hope, greed that digs the wells of despair. How few there are that create such sorrow for so many. The shock of greed shakes the homes of those who work to make ends meet. It buries the poor unseen. Dreams broken by those who always want more. Rise up voices of truth, let justice be proclaimed. Set right the balance that cripples the chances of working people. Bring low the selfish gods who rule uncaring and let greed's dark day be done.

**October 4**

Let the wings of God's compassion enfold you. Let them shelter you from harm, that you may find your rest, and the love that will restore you. No trouble is so great that God cannot overcome it. No hurt so deep that it will not be healed. Do not be afraid. Draw in the breath of the Spirit, for God is here until the shadows fade and the lights go on. Believe as you once believed, first faith in peace secure. Let the wings of God enfold you.

**October 5**

Thank you, God, for the promise of safety, but do not let me stay there too long. Push me out of the nest. Make me uncomfortable. Let me learn to fly on my own. Give me the confidence to trust the skill you have given me. Faith and risk are both the same, the call to test the limits, to create what has never existed before. Failure is only a lesson learned. Success an invitation to learn more. Give me the courage to try. Let me find heaven's horizon as I reach beyond my grasp.

**O c t o b e r   6**

It is a good day to live. They say my ancestors were unafraid to make the spirit journey when their time came, accepting it as a good day to die. I like to think that what made it so was their claim of every other day as a good day to live. Let me embrace each dawn as gift. Let me walk the hours of day unafraid, rejoicing in all I do, with grace and faith unbounded. Let evening find me close to those I love, warming my soul by the fires of their laughter. And let me sleep in a holy peace believing tomorrow will bring a blessing.

**O c t o b e r   7**

I want to say a quiet word to all who carry a quiet worry. How often we keep things to ourselves. We hold it in and bravely smile and soldier on and pretend we are fine, just fine. But fine we aren't and in time it shows to the few who know us best. To you I make a simple offer: hand your worry to me. Just for a moment. I am not God and cannot take it away. But as a friend I can carry it, just for now, while you feel life without its weight. I reach out with this quiet word: hand your worry to me. Just for now.

October 9

Look how far you have come. Even if the path that brought you here has been difficult, even if it took many unexpected turns, look how far you have come. You have the eyes of wisdom now. You have the experience to help many others. Your story rings true. Your experience offers healing to those who follow behind you. You would not be where you are if God had not been with you. Grace shines through you. It was not easy, but it was your journey, made and made bravely. Look how far you have come.

October 10

I am up early. I have to be at the hospital to anoint someone before surgery. I only have time to write what comes to my heart. Here it is: I cannot remember all of the pastoral calls I have made, the late night runs to the ER, the long wait in an ICU. There are too many to recall after all of these years, but one thing they all had in common. I never walked into any hospital room without finding the Spirit of God already there. Already comforting and healing. Already bringing peace and hope. I may be up early, but the Spirit never sleeps.

### October 11

God give me grace to learn from my mistakes. If I have any wisdom, it has not come to me as a reward. It comes from learning lessons gained by the experience of what I have done, good and bad. My mistakes have been my spiritual teachers more than my successes. But only because I was able to recognize my errors and be willing to start again. Give me the humility and courage to keep doing that. Help me to remember that in the school of the Spirit it is not important that I am always right. It is only important that I am willing to learn.

### October 12

Our roof leaks. The floors need doing. The sound system is old. The kitchen could use some new appliances. And none of that even gets us to the subject of mission, the dozens of things we want to do, plan to do, but wait to do because we just cannot afford it. God, when I went out to save the world you didn't tell me about this part. The budget meetings. The glamorous world of maintenance. The fun of fund-raising. No, you never mentioned this at all. And please, stop laughing. You know what I mean.

October 13

I will be at a funeral today for my own past. The widow of the man who confirmed me died, a gracious lady fading from view. I will celebrate her life on the very spot where her husband laid hands on me, welcoming me into the church. A circle of sacraments complete, a cycle of the Spirit made whole. I do not mourn so much as marvel at the way our lives dance through eternity. We move to music whose first chord signaled the birth of heaven. We turn on sounds that will not be heard for a million years. I have arrived without leaving. The mystery is the message.

October 14

Trust the vision God has given you. You alone are its steward. Each of us has been given a glimpse of the far curve of our own history. A wiser mind than ours weaves us into the future. Your vision is your handprint, your mark on days to come. It is that part of you that will abide, your gift long remembered. Do not doubt the power of what you see, for none but you can see it. Let it be a light to guide you to discover why you believed when believing was still young.

October 16

Could I get a clue as to where we are going? I know that you are navigating, God, and I trust you, but I could really use some better directions. Turn here, watch out, and don't go there are fairly vague. And please don't laugh. Saying we are on the road to glory is still just as vague. I need the big picture. The road map. I am always amazed where we go together, but I am never sure just how we got there. Can I get a clue? And no, please don't take the Book out of the glove compartment. I know it is helpful, but I can't read it while I drive.

October 18

Leave the shadows to do their work, drawing down the light of day. Let the fingers of twilight fold evening's cover over sleeping houses, where innocent hearts rest beneath a blanket of prayer. Let go of care and worry. They will wait patiently for your return. Walk sleep's solemn path, until God's holy dreams rise up around you like a garden growing by moonlight. In these innocent hours you will be a child again: safe and beloved, held by ancient arms, drawing down the light of day, gentle as nightfall.

October 19

I caught myself wanting to stop time again. It happens more and more. I go about my ordinary day and suddenly I have this longing to slow the clock, to keep things just as they are, if only for a while. I am an old man getting younger. I have learned again what I knew as a child. The air has a sweet taste. You can feel light in your heart. Animals have a secret language. Days are magic, nights are mystery. The younger I become, the more I want to play, just for a little longer, before I hear my Mother's call, before I have to sleep.

October 20

Cool our angry tempers, God, calm our sharp edged minds. Let us find common ground where we may listen to the heart of the other. Do not let our passions cloud reason or steal from us the simple courtesy of patience. So many hurts come when we forget to fight fair, substituting volume for meaning. Teach us to trust the power of shared ideas, of compromise and consensus. The path cleared by many hands is always easier to walk than the single trail of the one who walks alone.

October 21

I know how disappointment feels. I have carried its weight more than once. The disappointments we face can leave us empty in spirit but stronger in soul. God understands because God knew disappointment too: friends who ran away, a message ignored, betrayal and despair. God knows the shock of a life abruptly ended. You are not alone. There is no disappointment God cannot help you face.

October 23

S top thinking. Start feeling. If you are wrestling with a problem and it is winning, if you are weighing the evidence until you have broken the scale, if you have analyzed the analysis you just analyzed, then this playful word may be of use: stop thinking, start feeling. There is a loving presence that wants to help, if only you will trust the intuition given to you as a child. Feel the nearness of God. Feel God's strength surround you. Feel God's healing power touch you. Feel, so you may think more clearly.

**October 24**

I come to this hour to pray, when the Earth is still, the stars watching silently, a million lives sleeping around me. My prayers sweep out like a light across the sea. I know there are those who are lost in this dark, lost to life when life seems lost to them. I pray for the poor, the bereaved, the lonely, the dying. What help my words offer I do not know. I leave that mystery to God. My task is only to pray. I come to this hour to do so, a light seen on a dark sea, a voice to call an unknown name.

**October 25**

The end of time is not my charge, nor the ordering of the planets in their dance. I am only to be myself as best as I may be. To be true to others, to be humble, to stand for what is right, to care for the great and good Earth that gives me life. These are on my list of tasks and each one is demanding. I have more than enough to do. God bless me when I do them well, correct me when I go astray, gift me with what I need, and at the end, when all my work is through, bring me home to tell my story, the best as I may be.

October 26

Dark the road ahead and steep the climb before me, but in the distance I see a light. I keep my eye on that glow. I let it draw me, step by step, with confidence to walk in faith, even if sight should fail me. For no shadow may dim its promise, no threat steal its brightness. That light is the source of life, the goal of which poets sing, and mystics dream, the home of every heart born to believe. Come walk with me. Climb with me. Together we will cross the darkened plain to the light from which we both first came.

October 27

Economic justice is not a debate, but a truth on which our fate will be determined. Either we will embrace shared ownership of our financial future, or we will surrender that future to the desires of the few who horde the most. This is not the first time we have faced this moment. Riots and revolutions litter the road of greed, but this hinge of history may well be the most decisive. We will not elect the answer. We will not be given the answer. We will claim the answer when the people of God place the common good over the tyranny of privilege.

**October 28**

Take this cup from me. How many times have I prayed that? Life has no straight lines but a series of crossroads. It never gets any easier. Please, God, be with us when we have to do what we would rather not do. When we have to be brave. When we have to open an uncertain door. Give us courage, give us wisdom, give us grace. Remind us that we are not alone but ever under your watchful eye. If the cup cannot be removed, let us accept it with trust and do what must be done.

**October 30**

Give your heart to God, your mind to mystery, your hands to those in need. Religion is not rituals we perform, words we insist must be obeyed, the fancy dress we wear. It is how we behave when no one is watching. How we pray when we are alone. How we care when caring is the only reward. Eternity exists in the everyday, as familiar as the streets we walk. We may pretend we have ordered the infinite, but in God's realm love is our only currency and faith our passport to peace.

October 3 1

I asked a kindergarten group: can you tell me some of the things God made? The sun, the moon, the stars, they said, but one replied: and stuffed animals! I have a bear and I call him Pinky Bear. That's right, I said, everything is part of God's creation, and God cares for it all. For the sun and moon. For stars and sky. For little kids and big kids and kids who call themselves grown. The reach of God's love knows no bounds. It is love so pure it can only be described as the love a child has for the stuffed bear she holds in innocent sleep. God bless her. And God bless Pinky Bear.

# NOVEMBER

November 1

Can you hear them? Can you hear them as they pass by? Can you feel them standing just beside you? They are the ones who have gone before, saints who have touched our lives. They are the family to which we belong, ancient and never ending. Our ancestors watch over us, their constant vigil keeping. Their wisdom surrounds us. Their healing a river through channels of time. Can you hear them? They speak of a love they have seen, love beyond imagining, love that holds us safe, until we rise to meet them.

November 2

No more lonely hours, no more doubt or struggle. For this day shimmers in the light of the Spirit. It has been touched by hands that healed the blind, lifted up in arms that raised the dead. It is the day of salvation for the faith that would claim it. Stand up. Let old cares fall to dust around you. Stretch out. Be believing. See the light before you. This day is your new beginning. No more lonely hours, no more doubt or struggle. Not today. Not for you. This day is a miracle waiting for you to live it.

**November 3**

I have a comforting thought for any of us who had a dream that never came true. I believe that one of the gentle mercies of God is that God keeps track of these lost hopes. God restores them to us when we sit by the fireside of heaven. So if you never wrote that book, flew that plane, danced the ballet, got a blue ribbon or discovered an ancient civilization: you get your chance. You get your dream. Is this the sentimental wish of an aging priest? I will let you decide. As for me, I'm going to keep dreaming.

**November 4**

Here is a word to all faithful churches small and struggling. I know you wonder if you can keep going. There seem so few to do so much, with never enough money, never enough hands to turn the wheel of witness. But still you gather and still you sing. This word is a blessing from those who were just like you, the first church: followers of a voice calling them to come and see what only a few can do. They changed the world. Not with numbers, but with faith. Not with power, but praise. Not alone, but in the company of angels.

**November 6**

In these hard times I would like to start a bank, a credit union of grace. What God has given, I gladly invest, to be shared freely with those in need. Those who have prayed for work. Those who long for healing. Those whose hearts are burdened. They may apply for a loan of hope without fear of being turned down. The only catch is that they use the interest of their blessing as a tithe of mercy for others. My credit union of grace is open for business. Call it a bank of answered prayers. Call it community.

**November 7**

Siddhartha sat beneath his tree, waiting for an answer. He saw a path, four simple stones, across the stream of sorrow. He called the Earth to silence, casting compassion all around him, like cherry blossoms caught on the morning breeze. Should I look away from this good man because his words are not in my book? Can I listen to another voice to hear the echo of the Word I know? There is a garden of learning, where cherry blossoms catch the morning breeze. They drift down around Siddhartha, around the Shepherd, deep in conversation, pale pinks fans that catch the early light.

November 8

Simplify. Clarify. Sanctify. I have been thinking of how I can better order my life. These three words come to mind. To simplify how I live. To clarify how I think. To sanctify how I act. These are the first steps to a life of spiritual discipline. I share them with a prayer that we each be renewed by taking them. For it is in simplicity that we discover our center, in clarity that we hear our calling, in offering every act to God that every act becomes a blessing.

November 9

God be with me through this day, keep me close beside you, for I am not sure of the way, and may be lost if I walk alone. Let me be guided by your wisdom, sustained by your love, shielded by your Spirit. Let me not turn away from the straight path. If I meet others on the road, let me be grace to them in all I say and do, but if they stop their journey, let me walk on ever trusting in you. Let me travel lightly, my footprints soft on your creation. God be with me through this day, a traveler homeward bound.

**November 10**

I live a borrowed life on loan from God. One day my words will be forgotten. My voice an echo drifting on an ocean breeze. Images of me will be dust, my most precious possessions powder. Even those tied to me by the double helix will not recall my name or know from where I came. But I do not despair of my short span or wish my memory immortal. The One who loaned me this life will not forget. God will come to claim it, calling me by name, a borrowed life returned, redeemed by endless love.

**November 11**

When I was a child I thought of God as an old man, seated on a throne, making marks by my name. When I was in my twenties, God was a comrade in the struggle, calling us into the streets to demand an end to war. In my thirties God began to morph into Spirit, a mystic force of truth. In my forties God matured, a householder of heaven. Through my fifties God was Grandmother, ancient source of wisdom, constant source of healing. Now, crossing over sixty, I just smile. I have changed. God has not. We see the God we are.

**November 13**

Hail Mary, full of grace, blessed are you among women who know your story so well. Like you, they keep dreams within their hearts. Like you, they believe in hope when hope is all they have. Like you, they love in spite of loss, as though love was their last calling. Like you, when others are afraid, they hold community together, a light to see and follow. They are women of every time and place. Like you they are God's grace embodied, each one a miracle, each one the Mary she was born to be.

**November 14**

A woman once asked me, "What do I do if I cannot forgive someone for what they did?" She was a good woman and had been abused very badly. Hand your hurt to God, I told her, and in the meantime tell yourself that if you cannot forgive today, maybe tomorrow. That will leave space for the Spirit to get in and let forgiveness begin. "How long will that take?" I told her: I am grateful God did not put a time limit on forgiving me, so I won't do that to someone else. Maybe tomorrow. Maybe forever. Let God decide the time. You will know when the moment comes. Be gentle with yourself till then.

**November 15**

S ome handy definitions. Clergy are the people who wake you up when they stop talking. Laity are the ones who get things done in spite of the plan. The chair of the committee is the person who missed the last meeting. Bishops are people who pretend to be in charge while the community figures out what is going on. The liturgy is what we must never change until we do. The budget is a prayer. Vestries are kids who loved church camp so much they couldn't stop getting together when they grew up. The hymnal is a collection of songs we can't sing except for the ones we can. Pot luck suppers are what we do when we take a break from arguing and get back to being why we came to church in the first place.

**November 16**

G od send us leaders worthy of that name, women and men of virtue who do not look to short sighted self-interest, but to the needs of our people. Each day around us the dark tide rises, deep waters of poverty and war. The sick struggle to afford health, the worker to make a wage, the child to go to school, the soldier to turn toward home. Scandal smothers justice, rhetoric replaces truth. Honest citizens walk into a future they fear will be an echo of their past. I raise no partisan banner, but pray with one and all, change this history, great God of justice: send us leaders worthy of that name, while time yet remains.

**November 17**

How ancient is the dance between religion and magic. In ages long past we thought if we tossed a coin in a well we could win the favor of our gods. Now we Christians think if we belong to just this denomination or take just that communion God will like us best. I do not pretend to know the mind of God, much less to control it. But I do not think any God who could craft the stars would be much impressed by where I go to church. Let us be free of superstition and worship as we will, for denominations are but a suit of clothes. It is the one who is wearing them that concerns the God of all.

**November 18**

I stand within the circle of life. Above me the open sky, below me the ground of love. In four directions I recognize the compass that binds me to all living things. This is my spiritual gyroscope: the equilibrium of kinship. I walk in balance. I walk in beauty. I walk the seeker's way. I listen to the voice of my elders. I am family before I am me. I measure what I receive by what I give. This is the red road, ancient and profound, that leads to God's good medicine, to the camp of all my relations, the home of every tribe.

**November 20**

Thank you, God, for welcoming the stranger. Thank you for hospitality. I know it is one of your most ancient teachings. I will always seek to honor it, not because I imagine I may be welcoming angels, not even because it might be you. I will welcome the odd one out, the misfit, the outcast, the marginalized, the woman or man who makes me uncomfortable. I will welcome them warmly. Welcome them as my peer in your love. Welcome them as you welcomed me when I first came so nervously to your door.

**November 21**

Some people never start the journey. Some start but stop too soon. Some get distracted along the way. Some build palaces by the roadside. Some get busy helping others. Some try to organize the trip. Some lie in wait to steal from those who pass by. Some sell things to other travelers. Some open shrines along the path. Some die on the way. Some give birth. Some walk in laughing company. Some are grim. Some walk alone. Some sing, some curse. Some run, some crawl. Some teach, some learn. Some write words like these.

**November 22**

B e bold in what you believe, for God did not give you a timid faith. No matter how difficult the question, face it with the confidence of your conviction. Breathe deep the Spirit that surrounds you, stand on the rock of a Word certain, feel the hand of the One who made you on your shoulder. Illness, sorrow, conflict, fear: none of these can prevail against you. There is no hurt so deep that it can separate you from the purpose of God whose love overcomes every challenge. And if even for a moment your hope wavers, look around you: see me and ten thousand others, standing in prayer beside you.

**November 23**

M y mentor was an alcoholic. He was a man who had been so badly broken he almost died alone, lying on a floor. It was God who intervened that night. God pulled him back from being a statistic and turned him into a saint. This man was reborn through grace to touch many lives with his gentle heart and deep wisdom. If he did not tell you his story, you would never have imagined it. My mentor was living proof of redemption. He was a gospel walking. Never doubt that any of us can be saved from ourselves. God's love is the only change we need.

November 24

Each Thanksgiving my heart turns in two directions. I am thankful for all that God has given me, but I cannot help but think of those with so much less. I imagine you feel the same. Please join me in a prayer, a Thanksgiving tithe: thank you, God, for your many blessings, for your mercy and grace, but take a portion of what I have received and give it to those for whom this day is dark. Let them see your loving light and feel their hope restored. Let my thanksgiving be shared, no empty chair at your table.

November 25

If I could be the boss of you, I would give you a day off. Not a day off from work, but a day off from worry. I would give you the rest you need, the time you need. A day off from all that troubles you. But since I am not your boss, but in the same boat as you, I have an alternate plan: let's call in sick to the main office of anxiety. Let's find a place where we can skip stones across a pond beneath a cloudless sky.

### November 27

It is helpful to remember that the first followers, who we enshrine as icons of orthodoxy, were discontent seekers looking in radical places for new kinds of answers. Otherwise they would not have left the safety of their tradition, their morality, to see what was on the other side. They took the risk of listening to a different voice. They created a community of people from the margins of polite society. They upset authority. I doubt they would frown on any of us who do the same. Tradition is not only our past but what we create for tomorrow. Their example. Our choice.

### November 28

I suspect that you knew you were different at an early age. Not that you stood aloof or failed to find friends, but that you carried an awareness of life that was not easy to share. It was not just your outward sign, how you appeared to others, but an inward reality, a way of seeing, a sense that the air around you was scented with the fragrance of something sacred. And so you held your secret close, listening, waiting, until your time came, until your name was called by a voice familiar. You are what you were meant to be. You are called. You have a story that must be lived to be told. But I suspect you know that.

## November 29

Healing is transformation. It is spiritual chemistry that changes the substance of what diminishes us into the material of life renewed. It is process, either slow or swift, working its way through mind and spirit, reshaping what we thought permanent into what will grow. The catalyst is faith. From faith the flow of healing begins, releasing a power of good into all it touches. The agent of healing is prayer. We are physicians of prayer, sworn to practice its art for any who need a blessing. Let us be about our task, Spirit guided and Spirit filled, healing the healers, healing a waiting world.

## November 30

It is that season again. The time for being invisible. I do not share these words to darken happy hearts, but I speak to all those for whom holidays are a burden. I speak to those who feel some private hurt that keeps them from the joy they see in others. To any who understand my meaning, I offer a gift, small, but radiant in power. I hear your silence in the midst of singing. I see you unseen in the crowd. I have stood where you stand. You are not alone. You are not invisible. You are not forgotten. A single star shines above you, guiding love to where you are. It is that season again, your season, when God seeks the lonely place, to shelter hope where few would expect to find it.

# DECEMBER

**December 1**

At prayer this morning, beneath the clear night sky, I saw a shooting star, as bright as though it were drawn by the hand of a playful God. A sign in the heavens. A message of presence. I know enough science to explain it away, but I choose not to. I choose mystery. I choose meaning. I hope we all see the hand of God in the wonder of life around us. In wind and wave, in birds and branches, in shaded woods beneath high mountains. I hope we never fail to find the edges, the thin places, where God surprises us with the message: I am here.

**December 2**

Justice is not a thing made but a faith lived. Laws can be subverted, politicians can forget their promise. Justice has a deeper root, drawing its strength from the spirit of the people who uphold it. It knows no race or religion, but makes its home in every heart that honors the diversity of our shared dignity, the freedom of an equal chance. Justice rises when people embrace one another without condition to claim a common belief: how we live together is more important than what we have apart.

**December 4**

Avoice crying in the wilderness. The call of God does not come in the quiet spaces of comfort. It beckons us from wild places: that interior wilderness just outside the walls of polite society, the dark woods where we are afraid we may meet the stranger. It is the risky land of encounter. The invitation of God is to go out by going in. To question what we know. To encounter what we fear. We are baptized not with drops of water, but beads of sweat.

**December 5**

Fate is the blessing God has prepared for you. Destiny is how you receive it. We direct the course of our own lives. We control the path we take by the choices we make. Along the way God warns us of mistakes, offers a different option, sends us people who might provide what we need. At times we recognize these moments. Often we pass them by. In the end, we are the creators of our own story. Our fate is blessing, but our destiny is written by our own hand.

**December 6**

I have stood on the edge of a midnight canyon, where no friendly light warmed me, and called out our question into silent shadows: why. Why suffering? Why pain? Why the hurt that haunts our lives? Why the wrong that overwhelms the good? I get no answer, only an echo. I will go on asking why until the next generation of questioners takes my place. Suffering will not have the last word, not without challenge. We may not know the reason, but we will have the dignity of the question.

**December 7**

As I have grown older, my prayer list has grown longer. I have so many people to remember: people I have just met whose needs are new, people from long ago whose memory calls me to care. Though I spend these early hours alone I am never by myself. I am surrounded by a crowd of faces, all patiently waiting as I pray for them one by one. Through the dark glass of imagination, I also see men and women I will never meet, all waiting for the prayer I send them. Then as I amen my morning, I see you, and know you are praying for me.

**December 8**

God give us the grace to accept one another as we are. Few gifts have as much power for good as acceptance. Simple acceptance. It is liberation, the birthright of dignity. Acceptance allows every man and woman, every child, the right to be who God made them. No glass ceiling. No barriers by race or gender. No shame of sexuality. No class distinctions. No religious bigotry. No pretense. If we want to catch a glimpse of God's world to come we can do so very easily. Let others be what they are: a unique work of art come to life, made so by an Artist of endless imagination.

**December 9**

Like David with a sling, I go out to confront the illness that stands before you. It is called by many names, but its power remains the same. It seeks to frighten. It touches the body with pain. It forces the spirit into submission. It throws a family into confusion. It seems invincible. Illness is the giant in our midst. Like David, I step between you and what hurts you. Hand me one small stone of faith. Don't be afraid: watch what we can do when we trust in the One whose aim never fails.

**December 11**

By word and example. Some become so focused on word, on sharing the message, they slip into the pride of thinking their way must be the only one. Others focus so much on example, on living the message, they forget the reason they started in the first place. Tradition and social action are not opposites, only the ends of a balance bar. We carry the balance of baptism when we step out on the tightrope of faith. We walk our way by word and example over the water that defines us.

**December 12**

Spiritual vision is not the ability to predict the future. It is the ability to see hurt standing right before you. When the Messiah was asked, when will be the end of time, he answered, I have no idea. But he never walked by a person in pain. He never ignored children. He did not fail to see the money changers. Vision is the clarity of common sense, the perception of compassion. We are not great leaders because we promise what we pretend to see, but because we see what we refuse to pretend does not exist.

**December 13**

Come rest here beside me, here in this small space we have found for one another, where the chatter of an anxious world seems hushed, and the winds of worry are tamed to a gentle breeze. Sit quietly for a moment. Lay your troubles aside. They will be there when you leave. For now feel the blessing of just being, safe in a welcome ever genuine, at peace in the company of those who know you and love you all the more for the knowing. Come rest here beside me. Together we will watch the clouds teach us to pray.

**December 14**

How many people do you know who stay away from church for one of these reasons. Because they had a bad church experience. Because they believe they are spiritual but not religious. Because they think of church goers as intolerant and ignorant. Perhaps they are in your family or among your friends. These are good people from whom we must learn: learn how to heal deep hurts, learn how to share the mystery and let go of the lecture, learn how to open our doors. Our task is not to be defensive, but discerning. Our friends are trying to tell us something. What are we learning?

**December 15**

Feel free to file this one under Don Quixote, but I would like to see the national leaders of every religious community unite in a common public declaration: that we will hold our political candidates responsible for the content of their advertising. I have a suspicion that these coming months will see another sad display of political behavior where those who seek the highest offices in the land sink to the lowest depths of pandering. That is no way for a nation with dignity to conduct its campaigns. I think our spiritual leaders should ask for a pledge of civil discourse before the blood sport begins.

**December 16**

I pray this message for those who come to Christmas caught in a consumer culture that shames them if they cannot afford to buy all they feel they should. Hear the healing word of God: what you have to give cannot be bought. Your most precious gifts are the same ones Jesus gave to you. Give your time to those who need you. Give your forgiveness to those who hurt you. Give your love to all around you. You are the gift of God. You are the reason God came, and was born a poor child, and gave not as the world gives, but as only a generous spirit can give, the true spirit of Christmas.

**December 18**

Incarnation begins in humility. That is the first step in our own spiritual narrative. It is not feigned innocence or submission. It is what my ancestors believed was the essence of the holy: the sense of balance that holds a tension between pride and resignation, between limitation and possibility. What gave life to the sacred was vulnerable power. That same divine energy resides incarnate in each of us, if only, like God, we are willing to seek shelter in the poorest home we find.

**December 19**

If you collected all the sayings of Jesus into a single book, you would have a very small book. Why? Why so little recorded of what this great and brilliant thinker had to say? I have an answer to ponder. We always think of Jesus as the Teacher. We image him speaking to the multitudes. Speaking to the disciples. But what if he spent as much time listening as talking? Jesus the Listener. The wisest among us is not the one who does most of the talking. Look into the quiet eyes of a listener and you will find volumes of wisdom.

**December 20**

Peace on Earth. Goodwill to women who work two jobs, to men who come home weary. Goodwill to the soldier missing home, to the student anxious about tuition. Goodwill to the poor standing in line, to the elder sitting alone. Goodwill to the foreclosed family, to the pink slipped worker. Goodwill to those in chronic pain, to those in chronic hope. Goodwill to the hungry of body, mind or heart. Goodwill to those who have given up and to those who have just begun. Peace, I pray, peace, and goodwill to us all.

**December 21**

Sometimes the only truth I know is the love I see in your eyes. Like all frail people of all frail times, I have wrapped myself against cold history with layers of meaning. I have worn causes like hats, theologies like mufflers, class like a coat, gender like an old sweater. But still the sharp wind cuts through, chills the center soul I try to keep hidden. I am naked beneath the layers, knowing only one truth to sustain me. Love, I was told, love is the command, love the answer and love the shelter against all alarms. I look to you. Like a light your eyes lead me home.

**December 22**

The Christmas manger, the sentimental scene, the familiar cast of characters, on table tops and front lawns, all across America. This familiar image is a metaphor for my spiritual life. Sometimes I have been a shepherd, feeling called but not knowing why. Sometimes a wise man, surprised by my own intellect. Sometimes Joseph, silent but steady. Sometimes Mary, wanting to mother the world with unconditional love. Sometimes the camel, irascible in my convictions. Sometimes the donkey, willing to carry the load. And once in a great while, I am the infant, that holy hope, packed in straw, delivered by God, to a long waiting world.

**December 23**

Prayer makes a great Christmas gift. We can give it to every person on our list. We can give it to our family. We can give it to the people who bring our mail or pick up our garbage. We can make it for what we think the person wants most. We can afford it because it only costs a few minutes and we don't have to stand in line to get it or send it. A prayer is never returned, never put in the closet, never broken on the first day. We can wrap our prayers with fond memories, deep compassion, determined commitment, quiet faith. This Christmas we can give our gift of prayer. What better gift can we offer?

**December 25**

Once in Alaska, long ago, on a winter night, darker than any darkness I have known, the light I carried failed, and I was alone with that most ancient fear, the one that haunted us before there was fire. Disoriented, I knew if I walked the wrong way I might go on walking forever, wearing the night like a shroud. I prayed into the icy wind, sent out streamers of breath like a lifeline. Then I saw a light, a single light, a cabin light just beyond the trees. God is the light that comes to us just when we need it most, the ancient light that calms our fear, hope as old as fire.

**December 26**

Wisdom begins with a question. Love with a longing. Compassion with a need. Faith arises like seeds within the soul, where what is simple remains after all the explanations have fallen, a house of cards blown over by the breath of Spirit. Healing begins with a touch. Hope with a vision. Look to what you know, a truth in-born before beginning. Trust is built with experience. Community with just one person. Your heart learned an answer before your mind gave a reason.

### December 27

I see a world without hunger, where no child ever cries for want of food. I see the day when wars cease and people live without fear or hatred. I see the moment when racism dies. I see the hour when women walk as equals with men. I see the instant when humanity embraces its own diversity. I see the Earth reborn, the air so clear you can count stars in the heart of the city of God. I see God's promise fulfilled, God's love lived at last. I see all these things and more. I see because I believe.

### December 28

You have known moments when what you believed was so clear, it was like ice, sharp and clean and pure. You have also known disappointments so profound that they have numbed you with the blunt trauma of doubt. You have felt called. You have felt abandoned. You have seen healing. You have seen death. You have seen dreams fulfilled. You have seen hope slip through your fingers like sand. You have the patience of Job and the temper of Peter. You are proud. You are obedient. You are still here. You are a disciple.

**December 29**

Happy Old Year! Since I don't have a clue about what will be, I like to celebrate what has been. Thank you, God, for all the blessings of this past year, great and small. Thank you for the grace that got me through the hard times. Thank you for forgiving me for all the mistakes I made. Thank you for helping my family and friends, for your healing presence when we needed it most. Thank you for being alive and at work in the world. For watching over the poor. For saving lives. For the chance for peace. Thank you for a year of love past and a year of hope to come. May the good follow me forward and the bad fall far behind. Thank you.

**December 30**

This journey began almost a year ago. I was talked into joining Facebook. But I had no idea what to do. I have no family pictures. No grandkids. I have never traveled. Never been to Europe or Asia or the Holy Lands. I live the life of a monk in all but name. Not very interesting stuff. But I do have my prayers. I rise each morning to pray and meditate between four and six a.m. I decided to write out a few thoughts during this time and put them up on my wall. The handful of my Facebook friends were kind enough to read them. Now many of you do too. I don't know how long this will last, but I thank you for being part of it with me.

# AFTERWARD

## Afterward

As I was editing and revising these meditations, I read them over many times. While each meditation stands on its own, I did learn something by seeing them as a whole. There were some themes that began to weave together into a pattern.

First, if we are made of clay we should stay that way. Many of the meditations speak of resilience. Facing hard times, coping with illness, dealing with worry: these are the unavoidable realities of our lives. The spiritual response is not to try to turn to stone, imagining that our rigid theology or iron nerve will save us, but rather to be bendable before life's pressure. Humility, humor and hope allow our clay to take new shape, to adapt, to adjust, and finally, to transcend through God's grace even the most difficult passages of our pilgrimage.

Second, if we have a voice we should use it. Many of the meditations speak. Just that: they speak. They speak up, they speak out, they call us to a confidence of faith that does not remain passive in the face of injustice. The Word that we revere is not found in a book but in a voice. Our

## Afterward

shared witness to what is true, what is good, what is right makes a difference. The prophetic is not the partisan. It is the universal cry of the common person speaking truth to power. It is the vision of community translated into the language of change. To be silent is to be silenced.

Third, if we want love then we find love by giving love away. Many of the meditations are poems of praise, praise to simple compassion, to kindness, to being with another when just being there means more than anything else. Faith is not something we think, but something we do. It is not complicated or doctrinal. It is prayer, presence, patience. It is taking the time to care for one another. If there is any inspiration to be found in these pages, let it be the inspiration to never take love for granted, but to share love as broadly, as freely, as joyfully as ever may be.

# INDEX

# Index

## FEBRUARY

# HOPE AS OLD AS FIRE

## I n d e x

### MARCH

## Index

APRIL

HOPE AS OLD AS FIRE

**I n d e x**

MAY

## Index

JUNE

# I n d e x

## Index

# I n d e x

## I n d e x